INVINCIBLE

INVINCIBLE

THE 10 LIES YOU LEARN
GROWING UP WITH DOMESTIC VIOLENCE,
AND THE TRUTHS TO SET YOU FREE

BRIAN F. MARTIN

A PERIGEE BOOK

A PERIGEE BOOK
Published by the Penguin Group
Penguin Group (USA) LLC
375 Hudson Street, New York, New York 10014

USA • Canada • UK • Ireland • Australia • New Zealand • India • South Africa • China

penguin.com

A Penguin Random House Company

Library of Congress Cataloging-in-Publication Data

Martin, Brian F.
Invincible : the 10 lies you learn growing up with domestic violence, and
the truths to set you free / Brian F. Martin. — First edition.
pages   cm.
ISBN 978-0-399-16657-0 (hardback)
1. Family violence.   2. Victims of family violence.   3. Abused children.
4. Adult child abuse victims—Rehabilitation.   I. Title.
HV6626.M346 2014   2014013089
362.82'92—dc23

First edition: October 2014

PRINTED IN THE UNITED STATES OF AMERICA

10   9   8   7   6   5   4   3

Text design by Laura K. Corless

AUTHOR'S NOTE

Unless surnames have been used, all other names and identifying circumstances have been changed to protect the privacy of the subjects interviewed for this book.

This book is dedicated to you, the person reading these words. While we have not yet met I know we are connected. It is my sincere wish that what follows on the pages to come will help you or someone you care about unlearn the lies, embody the truths, and realize the hopes and dreams you have for your life and the lives of those you have the privilege to touch.

CONTENTS

Foreword by Tony Robbins xi

Preface by Renee McDonald, PhD xvii

Read Me First xxi

1   Undiscovered Gifts 1

2   Guilty to Free 27

3   Resentful to Compassionate 57

4   Sad to Grateful 83

5   Alone to Trusting 105

6   Angry to Passionate 125

7   Hopeless to Guided 145

8   Worthless to Accomplished 165

9   Fearful to Confident 181

10   Self-Conscious to Attractive 203

11   Unloved to Loving 221

My Wish for You 243

Acknowledgments 247

Notes 249

Index 254

FOREWORD

Over the past three decades, I have trained more than 4 million people, sharing with them many intimate details about my life. However, I have never shared the fact that I was a child of domestic violence. And, if I had not met Brian Martin, I don't know if I would have.

Brian asked to meet with me several years ago. I wanted to make time as I am always intrigued by what's behind the success of self-made individuals, and Brian's business was making waves in his industry. But on the day we had scheduled, I found myself running between meetings on a short stopover in New York before flying to London, and there was simply no time. Or at least that's what I thought until my assistant called to tell me that Brian had been waiting patiently in the downstairs lobby of my hotel for the past two hours. Someone that persistent I had to meet.

As it happened, I had about an hour before the car came to

take my wife, Sage, and me to the airport, so I invited Brian to come up to our suite. Immediately, it felt like we were on the same wavelength, members of the same tribe—and we had more in common than we knew. We talked for a while about his company and ways that he could help me reach my goals.

As I was getting ready to leave, Brian told me about the work he was doing through his foundation CDV—Children of Domestic Violence. He pulled out a report by UNICEF, and the numbers were staggering: 1 billion people worldwide are alive today who grew up living with domestic violence. I had no idea what a global epidemic this was. It resonated with me in ways I couldn't share with him yet. Sage and I were both in tears. Until then I had never told anyone outside of my immediate family that I had been one of those kids. It was a fact I would not publicly share until my interview with Oprah in February 2012.

I didn't like to talk about it much because my childhood does not define me, but I certainly grew up living with domestic violence. Like hundreds of millions of people, Brian and I grew up in households where violence was an ongoing part of our existence. We didn't call it violence then, we just called it life. Shouting voices from down the stairs, people smashing things on the wall, a fist through a door, those who you love most hurting one another, physically and emotionally.

I was on my own by the time I was seventeen. I used to live in anger and used my rage as energy. I converted it into drive, fortunately, because just being angry wouldn't have changed anything. Instead, those childhood experiences gave me the hunger to provide for my own wife and children, and the desire to help millions who've faced a similar situation. Feeling powerless inspired me to dedicate my life and career to empowering others.

That was also Brian's path, and the choice that countless others have made to reach their full potential despite their early experiences living with domestic violence. His story, and the many other stories you will read in this book, demonstrate that you don't need to start out in life with all the advantages. The difference between those who are successful and those who are not is psychological strength, emotional fitness. It's the capacity to face the worst setbacks and find something inside to push through and triumph no matter the circumstance.

In the following pages, Brian answers the question, *Can a childhood filled with violence and pain be transformed into one filled with strength, love, and freedom?* The simple answer is: *Yes, it can!* You have the power to shape the raw material of your past and mold it into the life that you want.

In fact, what appeals to me most about Brian's approach is that it is based on empowerment. Our experiences as children living with domestic violence have given us the equipment—a secret weapon if you will—to overcome all kinds of obstacles in our lives. What we went through, those things we faced *as children* have left us with vast inner reserves of strength, compassion, and courage. These are the gifts we were given in exchange for the price we paid as children. It means that we are *not* victims, we are victorious.

Like I have often said, your biography is not your destiny. We are not fated to repeat what happened to us ten, twenty, thirty years ago. At any moment in our lives we can choose which course we want to take. There's no reason to be stuck in the same story. It's just a question of figuring out how to flip the script.

But first, let's look at the facts. Let's see it as it is because this is not about positive thinking, this is about the truth.

Globally, UNICEF calls childhood domestic violence one of the most pervasive human rights violations in the world today, affecting a billion people worldwide.

What triggers this violence? Essentially, it arises when someone feels they have lost control: whether as a result of financial stress or the ending of a relationship or a threat to their well-being. Suddenly they snap. Why? Often those who commit violence—physical or verbal—are emotionally scarred from feeling helpless as children, and they have been filled with fear and rage. It does not often take a lot for a person in this state to be triggered. Perhaps her life doesn't match how she thinks it should be. Maybe she has a deep-seated fear that she is not good enough. And in that moment she loses control and starts to become violent toward her partner or children. This person (or perhaps you if you have been in this position) is in crisis and is now creating a greater crisis for those she loves.

Whether you have experienced abuse or you've been an abuser, it is important to understand that your actions and thoughts are often driven by falsehoods that you've learned—or often your parents learned. And that these falsehoods can be unlearned. You can create new truths. See it as it is; not worse than it is. The deeper truth is that no matter where you are in life, you have not yet tapped into your full potential. But it is within your grasp.

Like millions of others, we first experienced this pain as children, forming the memories and associations that shaped our lives. But then we realized that we could choose to tell ourselves a different story. We, along with millions of others, including presidents, senators, Academy Award–winning actors, Grammy Award–winning entertainers, business leaders, inventors, artists, and billionaires, also happened upon some important truths, and that has made all the difference in our lives. These truths, when shared, unlock an avalanche of untapped potential. Out of so much pain and injustice, something good must come, and it does.

If you've experienced any part of what I have described here, you know that one of the most agonizing feelings in the world is to have the people you love most in the world—the people who are supposed to love you the most—put you in a position to be hurt. For some, feeling you can do nothing to stop the abuse of others is equally excruciating.

When you grow up living with domestic violence, witnessing those you love tear each other down with physical and verbal blows, your brain doesn't know how to deal with that. This kind of pain is not like a cut or a punch. It wounds the mind, the psyche, the spirit. It is one thing to have physical pain that can heal, but spiritual pain lives deep inside your subconscious mind and defines your self-concept; it leaves an indelible mark. But one thing is true: Only those who have experienced extreme pain have extreme strength. Spiritual pain creates spiritual depth and strength.

Most of us are looking for something outside ourselves to blame for our situation rather than finding a way to take control of ourselves and maximize our greatest strengths. Giving up self-control leads to depression, anger, resentment, and all the other lies that Brian talks about throughout this book. But the fact is, we have a choice.

The history of humankind has been shaped by men and women who made it through enormous pain; men and women who, no matter what they experienced, would not give up. They found the courage to move forward. And the truth is, the same energy is in your spirit as well. Courage doesn't mean you *aren't* afraid, it means you are afraid but you do what is necessary anyway.

If you grew up living with domestic violence—or care for someone who has—remember that there are choices. There are countless people who have been able to reclaim their past and rebuild it into something that serves the greater good for the future.

The potential's inside of you now, so embrace the gift. It's time to share the truth, to speak the truth, to live the truth.

The courageous men and women you'll meet in this book have felt that pain. Some of us felt our mother's and father's pain as though it were our own. Others were once caught in this cycle, yet have successfully broken free. They have learned a way of life that's based on contribution, inner strength, and love. This path is available to you, and your road map is here.

—TONY ROBBINS

PREFACE

Brian Martin contacted me several years ago seeking my professional advice. He said he was committed to helping children living in partner-abusive families, and he wanted to be sure that his charitable foundation's programs reflected the best that science had to offer on the subject. I am often asked to consult on program development, but until that point I had never met an individual so passionate and so fiercely committed to making a difference in the lives of those who grew up living with domestic violence. Since then, I have watched and occasionally assisted as Brian has worked tirelessly to raise awareness of the fact that abuse of a parent is devastating for a child to witness and that the suffering of those who have grown up in these homes is widely overlooked.

Brian has convened scholars and authorities in the areas of domestic violence, mental health, and leadership to glean their wisdom; produced an award-winning documentary about the issue, and developed a campaign and online educational program to raise awareness and offer help for those affected by what is now known as childhood domestic violence. The Change a Life program developed by his foundation, available at cdv.org, is the first of its kind, designed to provide information and support for those who have grown up in—or who want to help someone growing up in—a partner-abusive home. I am happy to have played a role in the development and evaluation of the program and even more happy to call Brian a colleague and friend.

Brian contacted me because I have spent my academic career documenting and understanding the short- and long-term effects of domestic violence on children. Most programs designed to help children living in violent families naturally involve providing services directly to the child and/or the family itself. Yet there has been scant support and information to help the adults who were once those children.

This book, then, brings a fresh approach, using the knowledge gathered from decades of research to outline how those who were once children in partner-abusive families can reclaim their lives and futures. The science that informs this book, and the real-life experiences of men and women who have overcome the devastation of witnessing the abuse of a parent, together offer hope as well as object lessons for those trying to find their way forward.

There can be no doubt that early life in such an environment can shape how you think, feel, and act, especially in personal relationships and social interactions, and that these effects can be long lived. We've come a long way in learning how to help the children, but what about those who've already grown up and left their childhood homes? Many were raised at a time when it wasn't even acknowledged that witnessing violence could be damaging to a child. They have been left to struggle on their own, often too ashamed to share what happened with others. Because this issue has been under the radar for so long, they often don't connect the dots between what they learned in the homes they grew up in and the issues they face today. Some will insist that they are fine, even when the facts of their lives, such as depression, anxiety or fear, and abuse or failure in their own personal relationships offer evidence to the contrary.

Most are able to get away from the violence, yet they still may be unable to live the life they hoped to lead because their perceptions of themselves and the ways they relate to others are not as they would wish them to be, and they are unaware of that fact. The effects may not be so bad that their lives have been destroyed, but bad enough that the sustained satisfaction in relationships that others seem so easily to attain predictably escapes them. Their journey remains troubled.

This book distills the body of knowledge we now have on this subject and offers a hand to those who want to change their journey. Brian has crystallized on these pages all that those of us have learned and discussed with one another and shared with him. Whether you have been severely or only mildly affected by exposure to violence as a child, or just want to learn what it is like for others who have experienced it, these chapters will offer new ways to understand those experiences and a new perspective from which to view yourself and your relationships. Even a small change in perspective can transform a life.

Reading a book is seldom the total solution to a problem. But not everyone wants or has access to professional services or a trusted friend, and many are simply not ready to talk. For those who'd rather read quietly in a room and reflect, or at least start there, this is a gift. I could not be more proud to have been a part

READ ME FIRST

I know that dealing with the issues related to growing up with domestic violence is not easy. I applaud your courage and the fact that you have taken action and that you are reading this book to gain a better understanding.

From the outset, I wanted this book to present as complete a picture as possible of the emotional turmoil that I have seen—and personally experienced—in people who grew up living with domestic violence. While the first emotions I focused on were guilt, worthlessness, and fearfulness (as those are the feelings that have plagued me most), you may relate more strongly to others and be tempted to go directly to those respective chapters. But I encourage you to read through the book, chapter by chapter, as each one builds on the preceding one and you will inevitably find something in each that touches upon and illuminates your own experience. As a leading neuroscientist told me, "The brain seeks to find examples of what it already believes, whether those beliefs are true or not, helpful or hurtful."

At the end of each chapter you will find a summary, "From the Lie to the Truth." Once you have finished the whole book, I would urge you to go back to these summaries and perhaps focus on one exclusively for a week. Say the truth aloud to yourself in the morning and before you go to bed. Imagine yourself living the words throughout the day. Write it down in a place that stays with you. This is the truth for you and the more often you remind yourself of it, the more you will act as such until it becomes second nature. I have also included some simple exercises at the end of each chapter that will guide you to take one simple action that will create a habit, and the habit will create the outcome that you are seeking.

—BRIAN F. MARTIN

1

UNDISCOVERED GIFTS

I came to accept the secrets of our house as normal. . . .
I never talked to anyone about them.

—Bill Clinton, *My Life*

When I was six years old, my mother slept with a knife under her pillow, and I kept a baseball bat under my bed. It was one of those souvenir bats you might win at an amusement park, but it was the best weapon I could get my hands on. Although we kept these items hidden from one another and had no idea until thirty years later, they represented an unspoken bond we shared as mother and son—each of us determined to survive my mother's boyfriend.

Keith was a big guy who played football in college but was now a bartender. He came over to our apartment in the suburbs outside of Newark, New Jersey, four or five nights a week. I never knew when he would be there. I could never sleep on those nights, so I would sneak out of my room and listen to my mom and Keith from the top of the stairs as they argued in the kitchen. I felt so small and helpless to stop them. As they started yelling at each other, my heart would beat faster and faster. The fear and the rising tension almost felt worse than an actual blow—until my mother would scream. Most nights I would come down the stairs to try to stop it; sometimes I would stand at the stop of the stairs frozen in fear. I wasn't often the target of the violence, although at times I would get wrapped up in the confrontation. Occasionally, one of them would snap and take it out on me physically. This went on from the age of five until my late teens, when I finally moved out.

Those nights were a real-life nightmare. They changed my childhood forever and altered the person I grew up to become. They also changed who my mother was to become, and who Keith was to become. But not in the way you may think.

You see, my mother and Keith both grew up living with domestic violence. And so did *their* parents. They all grew up the same way I did. This was something I did not understand at the time; something I learned only a short time ago after finally speaking with my mother in preparation for this book.

YOU ARE MORE THAN YOU KNOW

My story is not unique. In the United States alone, more than 10 million children are living with domestic violence—just as I did, just as my mother did, just as Keith did. More than 1 in 7 adults in the United States, or 40 million people, lived with domestic violence as children. Worldwide, the number of people who lived with domestic violence when they were young is approximately 725 million. Another 275 million children are currently living with it. UNICEF calls it "one of the most pervasive human rights violations in the world."[1]

Perhaps you were one of them. Or perhaps you love someone

who grew up in a home like mine, or you know of a child in need of help. Or perhaps you are just a caring soul. Whatever prompted you to pick up this book, I am grateful that we are here together.

The simple but powerful message that I hope to share in these pages is this: If you lived with domestic violence when you were young, you no longer have to live with the *effects* today. As Alison Gopnik, professor of psychology at the University of California, Berkeley, says, "We are capable of change, but our childhood is part of who we are as an adult."[2] We will address what happened when you were young, but know this: Having grown up in that house, there are certain lies you learned in childhood about who you believe you are, and they may be holding you back from reaching your full potential and experiencing the happiness that was meant for you.

A friend of mine made me aware of the work of Dr. John Schindler, who defines happiness as "having pleasant thoughts most of the time." I love that definition because I can understand it. According to this description, I was not happy. I am now.

How about you? Are your thoughts pleasant most of the time? Or are you like I was, feeling more bad than good each day, but not knowing why? The awareness you'll gain from this book can take you from that place of feeling guilty to free, resentful to compassionate, sad to grateful, alone to trusting, angry to passionate, hopeless to guided, worthless to accomplished, fearful to confident, self-conscious to attractive, and unloved to loved.

For every lie I once believed, there is a transformative truth. And buried beneath all our childhood pain is a whole arsenal of hidden strengths—special gifts. That is our true unexpected inheritance. Because we survived difficulties that others never had to face, we have far more potential than we realize. We were forced to develop qualities of resilience, courage, and perseverance that are now readily available to us as adults. They are just below the surface, ready to be used to achieve whatever outcome we wish. These are the hidden gifts from our past that make us something more than strong. After what we've been through as children, there isn't much that can happen to us now that we're adults that can defeat us. We haven't killed ourselves; we're not in jail. We are still standing. Our lives have been so fire tested that, in many ways, we've become invincible.

I've taken this journey, and this is why I am excited for you. I believe that what lies ahead will help you discover your true self. As I have found, most people who grew up living with domestic violence are not who they think they are—they are much more. Think of this book as a simple guide that will lead you along the path to help you understand what you experienced, how it changed you, and how you can reach the potential that was meant for you.

But first things first—as Professor Kelly McGonigal says, "To build self-control you must first have self-awareness."[3]

WERE YOU A CHILD OF DOMESTIC VIOLENCE?

Who qualifies as a member of this silent group whose numbers are enough to populate an entire continent? Did your parents or those who cared for you hurt one another, verbally or physically? You were there, you saw it, heard it, you felt it. Even if they weren't physically hurting you, it felt just the same. Research is clear on this point. For a child, witnessing domestic violence is as psychologically damaging as being physically abused.

Did your parents scream at each other? To a child, that screaming can feel as painful and fearful as any physical blow. I recently met Crystal, a bright, beautiful young woman one year away from graduating from a well-known university. She'd grown up in a household where they used words and tone as weapons. Still today, she is fearful. She lacks confidence and feels that she is ultimately not good enough to become anything after she graduates. In an interview, I asked her: "When you were a child, how did you feel when your parents were screaming? How did you feel when you were anticipating that something bad may happen?" She replied, "I was fearful; I wasn't courageous enough to stop it. If I was good enough, I would have been able to."

Today, Crystal feels the same way she felt when she was a child in that house. She bases her experience as an adult on what she believes was true from the past. This is what we do. But of course, her self-image is based on these lies, so she needed to hear the truth. As children of domestic violence, why is it that we would allow the opinion of our parents to control our thoughts, feelings, and actions? When you look at it that way, isn't it silly to be so affected by the words and actions of people whose judgment you know to be questionable? Awareness of these simple facts is the first step to creating change. Crystal began to feel differently when she took control of her thoughts.

Did those who were supposed to care for you insult and demean you? As a child, there is no opinion as important as our parents'. What they say, we believe. Many adults who experienced physical violence in childhood will say that it wasn't the pain of the hand; it was the pain of the words that they remember most.

Or maybe you were part of the physical violence as well. About half of all children of domestic violence have been physically abused themselves. For many, it was not the pain of the physical abuse, but the pain associated with the feeling that they weren't able to stop it; that there was something wrong with them; that they weren't good enough. Personally, I would rather have taken open-handed blows to my face than have to watch the two adults in my home hurt each other and be powerless to stop it.

Whether it happened rarely or often, because it occurred in childhood, when our brains were developing, the impact can be dramatic and long lasting. In *The Boy Who Was Raised As a Dog*, Bruce Perry explains that even a "very brief stressful experience, at a key time in the development of the brain, resulted in alterations in stress hormone systems that lasted into adulthood. These early childhood experiences will have a far greater impact than later ones."[4]

WHAT IS THE IMPACT?

Living with domestic violence is physically and emotionally devastating, and the pain often stays with a child long into adulthood and often with dire consequences. These silent witnesses are, according to the UNICEF report "Behind Closed Doors," the "forgotten victims of violence in the home."[5] If providing everyone an opportunity to reach their full potential is a common goal, then we must focus on this issue. If ending domestic violence is a common goal, then focusing on one's experience in childhood is critical. Not least because, according to UNICEF, the single best predictor of children becoming either perpetrators or victims of domestic violence later in life is whether they grow up in a home where there is domestic violence.

These same children will grow into adults who display higher levels of depression, trauma-related symptoms, and lower self-esteem.[6] A sizable body of research has conclusively proven that childhood domestic violence—either observing or experiencing chronic, uncontrollable violence in the home as a child—causes cognitive and emotional damage that goes much deeper and lasts much longer than we ever previously suspected.

The chronic exposure to the stress of living in a violent home changes the neural architecture of a child's developing brain.[7] It significantly impairs regions that are essential for learning, memory, and the regulation of emotions. It actually lowers IQ and slows development.[8] In fact, prolonged exposure to domestic violence is no different from what soldiers experience in military combat, but because it's happening to a child whose brain is still developing, the results are often more traumatic and lasting. A 2011 senate hearing on the subject found that childhood exposure to domestic violence actually "changes who they are." As David Sousa, author of *How the Brain Learns*, told me, "It's virtually impossible for these children to realize their full potential as adults, unless they unlearn what was learned."

In December 2012, the Department of Justice released its "Report of the Attorney General's Task Force on Children Exposed to Violence," a groundbreaking study that has gone further than any other government agency to acknowledge the scale and long-reaching effects of living with domestic violence. The report calls this "one of the most significant challenges to the future of America's children we have ever known" and reaffirms what the research has been saying. "Living with domestic violence burdens children with a sense of loss and profound guilt and shame because of their mistaken assumption that they should have intervened to prevent the violence or tragically because they caused it."[9]

By now you may be wondering, "I am an adult now, not a child; I am in control of my thoughts, so shouldn't I be able to get over it?" According to Sousa, a part of the brain called the cognitive belief system controls what information we notice and what we let in.

"One of our weaknesses as a species is that we start establishing our beliefs as children before we can choose them as an adult," he explained to me in an interview. "They are often imposed on us by our environment early in childhood. Once we establish that belief system it serves as a filter. Your cognitive belief system, or your self-concept, tends to accept that information, which reinforces your beliefs and filters out information that doesn't."

So if early on in life you believed you were guilty, fearful, not good enough or unloved, then throughout life your brain tends to find examples to confirm that belief. *Why isn't he calling me back? Obviously it's because I am not good enough and unlovable. So here's another example to confirm what I already believe about myself.* This is how the brain works. We find more reasons to believe the lie. Do so often enough and it becomes the truth. You can't see it any differently.

WHY DOES NO ONE TALK ABOUT IT?

It's encouraging that governments worldwide are recognizing the alarming scale of the problem. Yet, shockingly, it remains almost entirely off the radar of our social consciousness.

So why has this epidemic been so widely overlooked from a public awareness standpoint? Domestic violence has very high awareness, but the impact of growing up living with domestic violence has very low awareness. Compare the awareness level to bullying, for example. No comparison. Why? There has been a general reluctance to talk about something that has been so stigmatized. And much of the focus of research and discussion has been on women in situations of domestic violence even though, as leading researcher Renee McDonald pointed out recently in an interview, "There are many more children in battered women's shelters than women."

Well, first and foremost, they don't know what to call it. People who grew up living with domestic violence struggle to define what the experience was. It wasn't domestic violence because that refers to adults; it wasn't child abuse in their eyes as that most often refers to physical abuse. Neither neglect nor emotional abuse adequately describe it. Many researchers will call it child witness to intimate partner violence. Have you ever heard of that? Less than 1 percent of the population has, according to a recent study. And further, this word "witness" doesn't work because it is a passive word and doesn't adequately describe the impact.

Children don't talk about it. They are afraid that if they say something outside the house, they may get into trouble. Or maybe they are afraid that one of their parents will get locked up, or they'll be taken away into foster care. Or maybe they will put one of their parents in greater peril.

One morning when I was in second grade, I woke up to screaming downstairs. I ran down and grabbed my mother by the hand and we sprinted out of the house in our pajamas. We kept running until we got to the police station. Later that day, Keith was escorted to a chair across from me in handcuffs. I don't know why this happened, but I do recall vividly what happened next. He leaned close to me and whispered, "Now I am *really* gonna hurt her." It is difficult for me to explain the pain those words caused in my little eight-year-old body, the degree of fear and guilt and worthlessness and hopelessness I felt. I caused it. And again, I would be unable to stop it.

Adults who are engaging in the violence don't talk about it for obvious reasons. Bystanders who are aware it is happening don't talk about it because it is *none of their business*. Besides the general silence, there's also a scarcity of resources available for children who are living with domestic violence currently or for the adults who did.

Fear and uncertainty also prevent them from doing the one thing that all research points to as the key step toward reaching their full potential—sharing what happened with another. Communicating our experiences helps us better understand what actually happened and its true significance, enabling us to gain an independent perspective from others. If there is no awareness and no sharing, how can we truly understand what we experienced?

As Dr. Norman Doidge, a renowned psychoanalyst explains, once we can understand and recognize the memory, we can file it as a past event and therefore rewire the brain to not pull it back up at any given point.[10]

For the billion people globally who lived with domestic violence in childhood and for the millions of children experiencing it now, this lack of awareness maintains the shame and isolation, prevents many from finding the help they need, and perpetuates the cycle of violence. Studies have shown, for example, that simply knowing the traumatic effects of violence on children creates a strong motivation for abusive parents to stop.[11]

Many parents and other caregivers in these situations simply have no idea of the far-reaching impact of their action, or inaction. Even the language used in all the research on this topic manages to lessen the public's already limited awareness. The studies and surveys use terms like *witness*, to describe those who've spent their early life living in these homes. What a weak word! It suggests that this is something we should be able to get over, as if we were just passing through. We know what this witnessing feels like, and it's far more than just being a spectator. It's that kind of bad branding—choosing words that not only don't resonate but minimize the true impact—that keeps this issue deep in the shadows.

This has resulted in a challenge that we all must face—how do we help a population that has fallen through the cracks: children who, as adults, are six times more likely to commit suicide, fifty times more likely to abuse drugs and alcohol, and seventy-nine times more likely to commit a violent act against another.[12] These are bright, creative, intelligent souls who grow to be adults who unfortunately never got to know their true selves, who feel more bad than good each day, but don't know why.

CLOSE TO BECOMING A STATISTIC

I could have easily become one of those statistics. Although I am the first in four generations in my family not to go to prison, I came close to repeating that pattern on any number of occasions and only now do I believe I am, each day, making progress toward reaching my full potential.

When I was seventeen I bought my mother a new car, with money I'd been making hustling jewelry. I'd just moved out of the house, and buying the car was my way of taking care of her. But I had a condition: I didn't want to ever see Keith there again, and she agreed. A couple of days later I spotted his car in front of the house. I pulled my car into the parking lot of an office building next to the house, turned off the engine, and then reached down under my car seat and pulled down the makeshift hiding compartment I'd created for my gun.

I held the gun in my hand and opened the car door with every intention of putting a few bullets in Keith. But as my foot touched the pavement I froze. I couldn't do it. Yet again I didn't have the courage to do what I tried to do dozens of times before. For no other reason than I didn't want to go to jail, and I knew I would get caught.

Furious with myself, I hit my head against the steering wheel again and again. What kind of man was I? I put the gun under my own chin. But then I found myself too afraid to pull the trigger. I was even a failure at trying to kill myself.

SOME DEFY THE ODDS

Anyone who has ever lived with domestic violence when they were young can relate in some way to my level of desperation. Two-thirds of all the young people in the United States who commit murder kill the person who is hurting their parent. That is a re-markable statistic. And even more remarkable when you think of all of those like me who never actually went through with it, but thought about it constantly. Even those who do not repeat the cycles of violence, incarceration, or substance abuse must often struggle with significant and ongoing emotional challenges, feel-ing more bad than good each day. This is not how it was supposed to be. Their lives are hidden tragedies of what could have been. Their relationships are not what they expected them to be. They feel that they are not good enough, knowing that they haven't reached their true potential in life.

Yet some come back stronger than ever. "More than any other creature, human beings are able to change," says Gopnik.[13] Their resilience and strength comes from having endured a childhood that others cannot even comprehend. Rather than fall into the cycle of violence, they reverse a childhood of pain and suffering to thrive, overcoming their difficulties, developing their talents, founding businesses, building communities, and creating lives for themselves that exceed their own hopes and dreams. For them, their childhood becomes the reason why they uniquely can.

Post-traumatic stress has become a familiar term, but the notion of post traumatic *growth* is not so common. It can, in fact, according to Stephen Joseph, be the engine of transformation. His research shows that this situation really can have a silver lining. "Adversity, like the grit that creates the oyster, is often what propels people to become more true to themselves, take on new challenges, and view life from a wider perspective," he says.[14] In other words, those who suffer the most change the world.

Some of the most accomplished people grew up living with domestic violence. As a child, Halle Berry watched her mother being brutally beaten by her father. Yet she was able to achieve a level of success in a field that is among the most competitive. It's hard to imagine such a beautiful woman grappling with low self-esteem, but she admits she's had to battle a sense of being unworthy since childhood.

"Violence was an ongoing part of my life," Anthony Robbins, the world-renowned life coach, remembers in a recent interview with Oprah Winfrey. "Something I couldn't escape. People smashing things on the wall, slamming the doors, putting their fists through things, being called a liar or having your head beaten up against the wall were all things happening in my house."[15]

Bill Clinton was terrified as a four-year-old, traumatized by violence in his home. But somehow he found a way to turn that fear into confidence—enough confidence to lead a nation.

The list goes on: Oprah Winfrey, Senator Scott Brown, Joe Torre, Patrick Stewart, Christina Aguilera, Drew Barrymore, Tina Turner, and countless others.

How did each of them find a path to resilience? How did they overcome their conditions and go on to accomplish great things in key areas of their lives? I became obsessed with finding the answers to these questions and, as I pursued them, other questions arose. What happens to people who grow up in homes like mine? They felt a pain that is unique to those who have seen the people they love most in life hurt each other again and again. At the most vulnerable point in their lives, they've experienced the emotional hurt of being powerless to stop it and having to anticipate it happening again and again. So, under those conditions, what makes them do what they do? How can they reach their full potential? The answers are simpler and more accessible than you might think.

ONE KEY TRUTH YOU MUST KNOW

As a child of domestic violence, you have inner reserves of strength far beyond the ordinary, and the ability to channel all that you have been through and felt into a life of extraordinary fulfillment and success. These truths are already inside of you, but you weren't born with them, you *earned* them by living through what you lived through and coming out of it to be here today. Again, it is what makes you invincible. As world-renowned psychotherapist Cloé Madanes told me, "People who experience an injustice in childhood, one brought on by their parents, feel a spiritual pain that shapes the unconscious. Because of what they experienced, they are able to reach a plane that few humans can, a level of understanding, resilience, and compassion that resides deep inside them." They felt a pain that is unique only to those who, at the most vulnerable moment in the life of a human being, know what it feels like to see those you love most in life hurt again and again and be powerless to stop it. All the while knowing it will happen again.

Wherever you are in your life now, it's possible to build on that resilience. You are precisely where you were meant to be. You have that power. Perhaps you endured suffering so others won't have to. So your children don't have to. Remember, "Resilient children are made, not born."[16] There is enough knowledge to help us make conscious decisions and unlearn patterns of thinking. These facts are "drawn from years of research and clinical practice [and show] that focusing on, understanding and deliberately taking control of what we do in our thoughts and actions can enable us to move forward in life following adversity."[17]

Findings reported only within the past two decades provide us with insights as to how the brain learns and have proven there are specific, concrete steps you can take to, as David Sousa puts it, "unlearn what was learned." We now know what works. The brain, Sousa says, is a pattern-making machine. Once it recognizes a pattern, a series of feelings are triggered. Most of these patterns are not identifiable or recognizable to us. They are hidden. But together we will find them and make a change.

In the same way that you do not have to be a computer scientist to work a computer, you do not need to be a therapist to know how to work your brain. As Bruce Perry points out, "Therapeutic experiences do not take place in therapy, but in naturally occurring healthy relationships."[18]

All of the evidence points to one clear fact: The pathway from living with domestic violence during early life to becoming resilient is shown through a caring, thoughtful adult who helped you unlearn what was learned, who showed you why you weren't guilty or worthless, and who let you see how you could become truly free and accomplished. I like to call that person the *One*.

Who was that One for you? Did you ever find her? Did he ever find you? Whether the answer is yes or no, the fact that you are reading this now, at this moment, answers the question for today. And today is what counts. Allow this book to be the One for you.

WHERE DO THESE ANSWERS COME FROM?

I wasn't aware of it at the time, but as I look back I realize my entire adult life has been about trying to answer the question, What happens to people who grow up living with domestic violence? I may not have been asking the right questions most of the time, but I was always seeking the answers. You probably have been doing the same.

It all started a little before the gun incident, when I was still living with my mother. She worked as a waitress, late into the night, and usually had a couple of cocktails to unwind after her shift. That's when she would open up to me with advice about how to be a better man or with admonitions like, "You're a selfish little prick, you know that?" which, at times, I certainly was. On other nights, it was, "My precious baby boy, my son, my son, my only son, I love you so much." I do not blame her for this, how could I blame her for what she did not know? How could I blame her for doing what she learned? She did remarkably well considering the childhood she had—a childhood very similar to mine.

On one of her two a.m. visits to my room she gave me a couple of books and said that she heard of them through the *Oprah Winfrey Show*. The one that struck me most was *Man's Search for Meaning* by Viktor Frankl, an Austrian neurologist and psychologist who survived a concentration camp during World War II and went on to establish a movement based on the premise that we can find and control the meaning in all forms of existence, even a concentration camp.

My takeaway was this: If Viktor Frankl could go through what he went through and control the meaning of what he experienced how could I not? He experienced more pain than I could ever imagine, and came through it to lead a productive and successful life and gave well beyond himself. He realized that he could not act or feel in a way that was different from whom he thought he was. So he controlled the meaning. One day I would be in control. I would have the knowledge. I wouldn't have to convince anyone of it because I would know it to be true. The rent would be paid and my mother would have a chance to live safely and comfortably, without having to work so hard or mask the pain with alcohol or cower in fear. We all have dreams and desires and we all want to experience life fully without limitations.

IF I KNOW THE ANSWERS WHY CAN'T I APPLY THEM?

With my newfound awareness, I immediately attempted to put Frankl's methods into practice. Not that I succeeded. At first, it was quite the opposite, which got me very discouraged. This was the wrong reaction yet again. One of my small slipups occurred during metal shop, my last class of the day. I wasn't particularly handy, but I liked the fact that there was a lot of free time in class for me to go through the sports pages of the *Newark Star-Ledger*. As I was poring through the pages that listed the horse races for the Meadowlands that night, taking bets from my classmates like some half-assed bookie, the shop teacher walked over to me and ripped the paper out of my hand.

"Brian, that is enough for today."

Of course he was right. I'd been handicapping for the entire period, and I had $50 worth of action on horses I knew couldn't win. But I didn't take it that way. In that moment, I believed my shop teacher was trying to make me look foolish. The rage I felt for all those times Keith belittled me or I felt belittled all on my own, rose up inside. I stood up, stared into his eyes and said, "You're right, it is." Then I grabbed my paper back and walked out of class.

No sooner was I down the hallway when I realized I had overreacted. I felt like a failure again; I had the information but didn't use it. I had just reread the previous night that I must control the meaning, and here I was doing the exact opposite. What was I, stupid? What I didn't realize at the time was that the sheer fact that I was trying was having a massively positive impact on my brain. As Doidge puts it, "Each time we try we begin fixing bad connections and creating new ones. Even just from the effort. We create new pathways in the brain, and we lay the groundwork for change. We may not be able to eliminate the feeling altogether, but we can choose not to act on it, and by making that choice, we heal."[19] Of course at the time, while hiding out in the bathroom smoking, I did not realize that and was not congratulating myself on recognizing my mistake. Instead, I was brought down to the guidance counselor's office, where I received additional answers.

YOU CAN CONTROL YOUR THOUGHTS LIKE YOU CONTROL YOUR FINGER

I told the counselor about Frankl's book and the disappointment I felt in myself for failing to control the meaning. She was impressed. Although I'd never considered college an option, and it was late in the day to start applying, she talked with me about the possibility and what I would need to do to get there. It was the first time an adult saw the possibility in me of becoming something more—a way to become financially successful beyond the hustling that was part of my youth. Then she gave me another gift: a copy of *The Seven Habits of Highly Effective People* by Stephen Covey.

While reading the book I came across a simple concept that I have seen hundreds of time since but, up until that time in my life, had never considered. Between a stimulus and a response there is a gap in time. What you choose to do in that gap makes all the difference. Covey had built on this idea from Viktor Frankl. I realized that a thought triggers a feeling and while I may not be able to control a given thought that strikes me, *I can choose what to do with that thought* in the same way I can control what I do with my fingers or hand or arm. "Noticing a thought is not the same as believing it," says Kelly McGonigal.[20] Or, as educational psychologist Kristin Neff, puts it, "Mindfulness requires that we not 'over identify' with thoughts and feelings, so that we are caught up and swept away by negativity."[21]

So I could choose to buy into the feeling and stay with it or choose to get out of it. It struck me enough to write on the cover of my school notebook, "Manage the Gap." And as I write these words I am looking at a small plaque on my desk that has the same message. Simple statements that present you with a new possibility, with a new truth, can create immediate change. In other words, as Frankl instructs, instead of just reacting, use that moment between feeling and action to step outside of yourself and ask some basic questions (manage the gap), then choose the answer that will lead to the most positive action (control the meaning).

APPLYING THE ANSWERS LEADS TO AN IMPORTANT QUESTION

In my final year of high school I worked hard to get my grades up and got into a county college. It was there that I met Stacey, the woman who was to become my wife.

I did not believe that I was naturally smart. This is a belief that I share with other people who grew up living with domestic violence. How could I spend time thinking about school when I was busy running to the police station in my pajamas? How could *you*? Didn't you spend most of your time in school trying to figure out what your classmates and teachers were thinking about you? Perhaps worried about what the night would bring? How could we pay attention? Thus we were made to believe we weren't smart, and our brain found evidence to support it. It's another lie that we will unlearn during our time together.

But I was determined to make it. I did well enough to get accepted to graduate school and get an MBA, after which I married, started a family, and got a good job. Then I took a risk to start my own business and built a successful company that would give me, my mother, my wife, and my children the kind of financial security that I had craved when I was growing up. By the time I hit my late twenties, early thirties, my life revolved around work. I wasn't as close to my wife and children as I thought I should be, but I believed I was doing it for them. And besides, I was good at it. This was an area of my life where I had complete control. I kept on reading and learning—for the purpose of getting better at my profession, which would lead to more money, to more security, and ultimately to the power I never had when I was a child. Now *I* would be the one who was important. Or so I thought.

One day during a meeting at Nickelodeon, their executives shared a fascinating statistic: When parents were asked to name their fondest childhood memory, the vast majority said, "Memories of my time vacationing with family." As I thought about that later that night, I asked myself, "What were *my* fondest childhood memories?" Well, most of the ones that I remembered all sucked. But why should that have to be the case for others who grew up in the same way I did? So, in 2007, I decided to create a foundation called Makers of Memories, which provided trips for children who shared my background of living with domestic violence. I saw the excitement in the eyes of my young son and daughter when I took them on trips and exposed them to new discoveries, so I thought it would help create joyful memories for kids who grew up like me.

At the end of one trip to Walt Disney World in Florida, we all watched a spectacular fireworks show called "Wishes" that ended with Jiminy Cricket singing, "When You Wish upon a Star." At the end a star is shot over Cinderella's Castle and you are supposed to make a wish upon it. I mentioned that to the six-year-old boy sitting next to me and then asked him, "What's your wish?"

He looked up at me and quietly answered, "I wish they would stop hurting each other." I put my arms around him and just sat there in silence. Of course, when I was six that would have been my answer too.

This should not be the wish of any child. But there it was—a young life filled with nightmares. If he couldn't dream at that moment in life, when could he ever dream? He needed a dream to get through the nightmare, and I didn't deliver.

WHAT CAN HELP THOSE WHO GREW UP LIVING WITH DOMESTIC VIOLENCE?

I was haunted by my conversation with that child. It bothered me that our foundation's mission wasn't having the kind of impact I'd hoped for. So in the days following that Disney trip I started intensively researching and came across "Behind Closed Doors," the UNICEF study on children of domestic violence I cited earlier. That night I reread the short document about thirty times. I was blown away by the size and scope of the problem and that, despite the sheer numbers—hundreds of millions—who'd lived or were still living with domestic violence, among the general population there was almost no awareness of these facts. I knew that I wanted to get word out to all these children and to adults who were once these children. I wanted them to understand that they were not alone and that they could reach their full potential in all areas— socially, professionally, financially, emotionally—in all the ways that mattered most to them.

Of course, I'm no expert. I'm just a guy who's lived through this and didn't want others to have to suffer under the same legacy. Because I'm not an expert, I reached out to those who were.

GREAT MINDS COME TOGETHER

In 2010, we hosted a summit of academics, neuroscientists, and researchers to figure out promising ways we could use their knowledge to help the billion people across the globe who grew up living with domestic violence. My original intent was to film this gathering as part of a documentary, to raise awareness. Several ideas were discussed at the event. But a key question was: What creates resiliency? Some people who grew up living with domestic violence do better than others, and the information we shared led us to the conclusion that the most resilient among them have had an adult who stepped into their lives—a teacher, relative, or friend—who reinforced truths and helped them unlearn the lies.

These findings eventually led to our foundation's alliance with UNICEF and the world's leading scholars to develop and implement the Change a Life program, a scalable solution that trains adults to elevate awareness and deliver key messages to those still living with domestic violence, to help change a life.

It was a productive day—many of them had never met one another.

As the session was coming to a close, I asked a few questions that had been on my mind for a long time: How do people who've grown up living with domestic violence feel? What do they believe about themselves? What feelings do they experience most frequently? The group put forward a number of ideas but the words most often used were *guilty, resentful, sad, alone, angry, hopeless, worthless, fearful, self-conscious,* and *unloved.* These are, in fact, the ten lies you learn growing up with domestic violence—lies that you can unlearn after you uncover the truths.

It was another, pivotal moment; a major breakthrough. That night I didn't sleep. I studied my notes well into the next morning. For all my studying and reading; for all my awareness of childhood domestic violence as a problem and my desire to do something about it, I had not been self-aware. But there it was with every emotion, I realized that I *believed* each of these lies about myself. Deep down, no matter what I portrayed to the outside world, I believed I was and was destined to always be guilty, resentful, sad, alone, angry, hopeless, worthless, fearful, self-conscious, and un-loved. These beliefs shaped all of my thoughts, which created my feelings, which then led me to act. Many of those actions kept me from reaching my full potential.

All those books I'd been reading for most of my adult life really weren't helping, at least not in the way they were intended. How can a self-help tactic work when deep down you believe all of these things and you feel far more bad than good each day? After all, our feelings and actions are always consistent with who we think we are. Who you believe you are, you are. That is your self-concept and you cannot put a self-help tactic on top of it. You need to address the root of the issue first: the self-concept.

But as we have learned, we can unlearn what was learned. "The brain is plastic and is changing all the time. With focus, recognition and motivation we control how our brain functions," explains Doidge.[22] You can unlearn the lies you learned in childhood and form new ways of thinking. You take a small action that builds a habit and the habit gets the result.

Yes, change can be automatic. For some it may not; but one thing that can happen immediately is awareness. More than 80 percent of change is awareness! That awareness leads to progress, and daily progress leads to living the life that was meant for you—the one that was stolen from you as a child. Changing the story of our lives can take time or it can happen in an instant, but prog-ress is happening right now. It is all well within your grasp.

IT'S WORTH IT

One change will create momentum. You will begin finding rea-sons why you can, as opposed to why you can't. For many, simply reading these words, or even just relating to the examples of others, can be the first step in a broader transformation. As you unlearn the lies that were unconsciously encoded when you were a child and free yourself from them, you can begin a journey toward reclaiming the life you were meant to live.

Any of us can change the story of our lives. We can create new memories and new emotional habits that will replace the old ones. By erasing that glitch that was corrupted by environments and behavior not of our choosing, we *can* give ourselves, and those around us, a better life.

As a child, your most fundamental need, security, was not met. You felt powerless, unimportant, and insignificant. But the fact is you are incredibly accomplished, important, and powerful. You are not broken. You endured so much *as a child*, and yet you are here. You already paid the price, and yet you are here. But it doesn't stop there. You may not be tapping into that deep well of knowledge and strength that you possess, you may not even realize it's just below the surface. There's so much more of life out there for you to live, so it's time to take it back and do what you were meant to do; be who you were meant to be. The tools in this book will provide you with the guide to get there and to build on all that you have already achieved.

LEARNING FROM THOSE WHO CAME BEFORE US

This book brings together the wisdom and experience of many people who have already spent hundreds of thousands of hours studying what happens to people who grow up living with domestic violence. I have tried to summarize some of the most effective tools and strategies to create change so you can realize what you were meant to experience in this life—your dreams and desired outcomes (not goals, because goals are hopes and outcomes happen). So take this journey with me and receive this genuine message of possibility, delivered through the authentic voices of those who have successfully fought hard against the darkness. Their stories may not be complete. We all have more growing to do, but we are now moving toward our most important desired outcomes, as opposed to away from them and doing so happily. Our thoughts are pleasant most of the time.

Even if you didn't get those same opportunities, even if you haven't been able to change your environment or encountered someone caring and insightful enough to intervene and help you see through the lies, you have the power to take those first steps on your terms.

Anyone can create the life he or she desires. You too can join the ranks of courageous men and women who have decided to see themselves not as victims but as whom they really are—free, compassionate, grateful, trusting, passionate, guided, accomplished, confident, attractive, and loving. Your time is now. You deserve this; your loved ones deserve this. This was who you were meant to be.

2

GUILTY TO FREE

The worst guilt is to accept an undeserved guilt.

—Ayn Rand, *Atlas Shrugged*

Embarrassment, a sense of culpability, a feeling you should have been able to stop it, shame because there is something inherently wrong with you, humiliation, remorse, even the sense that you were somehow the cause—these are all variations of one of the biggest and most pervasive lies we tell ourselves after living with domestic violence during early life—that we are somehow guilty or that we have something to be ashamed of. That it was *our* fault. As Rick Warren, author of *The Purpose Driven Life*, writes, "Many people are driven by guilt. They spend their entire lives running from regret or hiding their shame. Guilt driven people are manipulated by memories. They allow their past to control their future."[1]

Part of the problem stems from the underdeveloped logical thinking centers in the developing brain, which lead children to create impossible childhood expectations—like summoning magic powers to make things better or being able to protect a parent by challenging an adult three times their size.

"When you're young," neuroscientist David Sousa explained to me recently, "the neocortex, which is responsible for rationale thinking, is still growing. Our instinctive, emotional limbic system just outguns the kind of logical, rational thinking that might come from a more mature neocortex. As a result, children cannot rationally understand their situations as an adult can. Out of desperation to protect their parents, they invent impossible ideas. And when they can't live up to their imaginings, children feel horribly guilty."

Later in life, that guilt and shame simply become fact and they hold us back in so many ways. They are heavy burdens that slow us down and stop us from taking action, an invisible bondage that weakens willpower. We start something, then fail or quit, only to reinforce that sense of blame. Finally, we give up. We don't even try, becoming prisoners of this lie.

As bestselling author John Bradshaw writes in *Healing the Shame That Binds You*, "Abuse creates toxic shame—the feeling of being flawed and diminished and never measuring up. Toxic shame feels much worse than guilt. With guilt, you've done something wrong; but you can repair that—you can do something about it. With toxic shame there's something wrong with you and there's nothing you can do about it; you are inadequate and defective. Toxic shame is the core of the wounded child."[2]

But there's a way to break these bonds of guilt and shame— action. Action is freedom made visible. Freedom is not something you can actually see, but those who are free—free of guilt and shame—choose to use their freedom to take action in ways that move them closer toward their full potential.

As someone who has lived with domestic violence as a child, you started out with tremendous resolve. You, like so many of the men and women you will meet in this book, had the courage to take action and deal with situations beyond the imaginations of most adults. But the layers of untruths you learned as a child cancelled that willpower along the way.

That was the case for British actor Martin Rayner, who was so consumed with guilt and shame over not being able to stop the violence in his home that he became physically ill, spending much of his boyhood barely able to lift himself off the couch.

When I asked him to describe his childhood in post–World War II England, Martin doesn't hesitate: "Bleak."

Born into a home plagued with violence, Martin was mentally and physically crippled by shame and guilt stemming from the poverty, violence, and neglect that defined his circumstances. For him, the memory of not being able to prevent the violence between his mother and his father was by far the worst.

His parents, who were childhood sweethearts from an industrial and coal-mining region in the middle of England, came from a working-class background that was steeped in ignorance and superstition.

It was a time and place of gas lamps, horse-drawn carts, coal soot, and violence in the home that was never talked about. Ever wonder where the phrase "rule of thumb" comes from? An archaic British law that allowed man to beat his wife with a stick no wider than his thumb. What a man did in his home was nobody's business.

Except that in Martin's house, it was the reverse: his mother viciously beat his father. As Martin remembers it, she suffered from violent mood swings, exacerbated by her menstrual cycle. As a girl, no one told her about her body and what would happen when she went through puberty, so when her period first came, she screamed uncontrollably, believing she was dying, or cursed, or both, and she never got over the trauma and no one stepped in to help her understand. There was probably more to her up-bringing that left her scarred and prone to violent outbursts, al-though the violence was rarely directed at her children.

She attacked Martin's father, with knives, broomsticks, coat hang-ers, or whatever else she could get her hands on, as Martin watched, horrified. In the eyes of Martin, this frail, almost effeminate man was a saint. It wasn't until later that he realized his father was a full participant in the dysfunction, taunting and manipulating her with insults out of some twisted desire to appear like a martyr. He delib-erately provoked her, hoping her fury would lead to an attack.

For their children, these scenes were deeply painful to witness. On some level, Martin felt responsible, and it pained him that he couldn't do more to protect his father. Although Martin, his brother, and his sister were rarely at the receiving end of their mother's physical blows, her verbal threats, screams, and insults were a constant, especially when Martin would try to intervene to protect his father by jumping on his mother's back to pull her away.

Not that he was much of a match for his mom. Health prob-lems, including ulcers, severe constipation, and malnutrition plagued Martin as a young boy, causing intense physical pain and frailty. He was so stressed that he had trouble swallowing his food. School lunch was a torment, because if he was spotted wasting food he'd be punished, and yet he sat at the same table as the head of the school. "It was a fearsome thing to do, so I had to go through the motions of chewing my food, and then spit it into a handkerchief when he wasn't looking."

His digestion was so bad; he had to excuse himself from class to hide in a closet.

"I didn't know what to do with myself; I couldn't go to the bathroom and I couldn't swallow. I was a mess," he told me. It is not uncommon for people who grow up with domestic violence to suffer ill-health as we will learn later.

THERE WAS SOMETHING I COULD HAVE DONE

At five, Martin moved with his family to southern England, where his father found work as a hall porter at a mental hospital. The irony was not lost on Martin, even then. "We had our own madhouse."

The institution provided modest housing for the working families on the grounds, and gardens where they could grow their own vegetables. But even with that help, there was nothing left to pay the bills. His father earned so little and was so deeply in debt from a failed business venture, that they were barely able to survive. Back in those days, everything was delivered to the home— milk, coal, even bread—and the tradesmen would come knocking every week to collect their fees. Martin and his siblings were told to stay away from the windows and hide when they heard the clacking of the horse's hoofs—a warning that the bill collectors' horse carts were approaching the house. Entire afternoons were spent with the lights out and the curtains drawn while various angry men banged on their front door.

"It was terrible for us kids, because we developed the idea that the whole world was after us and we were not acceptable," Martin recalls.

Martin was so ashamed of his living circumstances—the filthy home littered with broken furniture and wallpaper that stopped at the top of the sofa—that when his school friends came calling he never invited them in.

"The idea of someone coming in and seeing what my life was really like was so awful to me that I would even keep my best friend talking at the door," he recalls. "I felt I had a part in what was going on, a part in a family that was no good."

Even worse was what Martin describes as "benign neglect," based on ignorance, poverty, and extreme dysfunction. Martin wanted to die from embarrassment when his older brother, who was deeply disturbed, used to change his trousers in the middle of the living room, in front of company. It was as if they had been raised by wolves. The children didn't even own a pair of underwear or a toothbrush. It all added to Martin's profound feelings of guilt and shame.

IT WAS MY FAULT

Martin felt responsible, as if his parents' ignorance and neglect was *his* fault. As Sousa explained in our interview, it's hard for an adult to understand why a child would feel this way because as an adult we have a fully developed rational brain. But what drives a child of seven or eight is their emotional brain, which is the part that is fully developed by then. So "if they are present and it's happening or they cannot stop it, they can very easily and often conclude it is their fault or that there is something wrong with them," he says. It can lead to depression, social withdrawal, and all kinds of damaging internalization, resulting in Martin's childhood ulcer, for example.

Physical effects are not unusual. According to the research, over the long term, induced feelings of guilt or shame may even cause immunological problems, and inflammatory conditions. A recent study by the department of psychology at the University of California, Los Angeles, found that participants in a condition of self-blame showed increased levels of pro-inflammatory cytokine activity, those molecules or antibody proteins associated with cell signaling to promote an immune response. In other words, prolonged guilt can potentially bring about a host of chronic, stress-induced diseases if we don't get it under control.

As James Pennebaker professor and chair of psychology at the University of Texas recently discovered in his research, keeping these experiences locked away inside you, never discussed, can do even more harm and may even be more damaging than the actual traumatic event.

It is an extraordinarily traumatic event for a child to see his or her parent get hurt. As Renee McDonald, a leading childhood domestic violence expert and associate dean at Southern Methodist University, explains, children's nervous systems are acutely attuned to their parents. Mirror neurons, which under ideal conditions are designed to help children feel empathy and learn imitative behavior, instead deliver suffering. The child actually feels physical pain just by observing the violence inflicted on a loved one and learns to feel a twisted kind of empathy—guilt.

Behind most childhood feelings of guilt is the conviction that the child could have changed the outcome. Many secretly hold on to this belief for the rest of their lives. But the simple truth is that it is never the fault of someone who grew up living with domestic violence. They are never to blame. Any guilt they inherit is a lie.

Children can never control the actions of an adult; nor should it ever be expected of them. But this truth is rarely shared with children and by the time they become adults the lie is so established, it goes unquestioned. It's just who they are. When they were young, they needed to be told the truths and if they were not, then they had no way of unlearning what was learned.

SHARING THE TRUTH THAT WE COULD NOT SEE

Sometimes it takes another—an adult outside the situation, to reveal the truth. That was the case for Martin. As much as school was a struggle for him, at a prize-giving ceremony he was shocked to hear his name called out. He was asked to come to the stage, where his headmaster shook his hand and gave him a book with the inscription, "For Cheerful Helpfulness." Others had recognized his kind and compassionate spirit, his willingness to pitch in and help others despite the misery of his circumstances. Thankfully, Martin had a couple of affirming moments as a child—just barely enough positive reinforcement to keep his inner light shining and put him on a more hopeful path. "Until then," he says, "I'd had no awareness of myself in this way."

That truth helped set him free. It was one of several moments in a process that lifted him out of guilt's grip.

He began acting in ways that filled others with love and happiness. On some subconscious level, he was trying to create a world that was the exact opposite of the one he was living in. He was given a reputation to live up to.

At eleven, another moment came. He then began looking for examples of why he was free from the guilt—ways that he could express himself. And his brain began finding evidence of why it was true. In the English school system students finishing up primary school took a life-altering exam known as the eleven-plus, which determined whether a child went on to a grammar school, which could give them access to a university education, or was to be enrolled in a technical or a general education school. In his isolation, Martin knew nothing about the exam until a friend happened to mention it. With just a couple of weeks to study for something the other kids had been preparing for over months, Martin passed the test, something no one else was expecting of him. Because he believed he could and because he thought he was worth it, he felt free and took action.

"Well that's a surprise, but a nice surprise I suppose," his father said, rewarding him with some toy soldiers instead of a badly needed school uniform.

But on his first day of grammar school, Martin was plucked out of class and told that his mother, who'd been suffering from cancer, hardened arteries, and several other serious health problems, had died at age forty-three. His father was inconsolable, wailing beside her coffin like an infant and forcing his children to participate in a séance, standing by their mother's open casket as she lay in wake.

"The idea that this waxen figure lying in a casket was talking to us was just mind boggling; I had nightmares for years after that," recalls Martin.

Seeing that Martin's father was in no mental state to take care of his kids (not that he ever was), Martin's Uncle Chick took them into his home, buying them their first sets of underwear and tooth-brushes, introducing them to the basics of personal hygiene and personal care, and giving them a glimpse of what life could be.

"He became a sort of hero to me; my beacon in the storm."

For a moment, Uncle Chick became yet another One, helping Martin see the truth. While the amount of time Martin's uncle and teacher spent in Martin's life was brief, it was enough to reinforce the truth and reverse the lie of guilt and set him free. An inner flame was lit, and Martin vowed he was going to leave to pursue a career in acting as soon as he was old enough to strike out on his own.

At age nineteen, he took a job polishing brass and cleaning toilets in a theater in London's West End, where he quickly learned that was not the correct path into acting. A year later, to save money for drama school, he headed south, to the Isle of Wight, a tiny tourist island in the English Channel, and took a job in a restaurant. Martin thrived in his new life, eating well, swimming, and being outdoors. Physically, he transformed from a "puny, pale, nervous thing," to a strapping young man.

HIS CHOICE TO TAKE ACTION

Emboldened by his newfound strength and energy, he moved back to London to start his training at the Drama Studio. But for the first year he wouldn't even act. That old reflex of shame and shyness was holding him back.

"I just assumed that everyone else was better than me and I couldn't act."

Old beliefs sometimes come back to us when we are facing key challenges. When we are in doubt, we go back to what we know—the lie. But Martin unconsciously knew the antidote—action!

He kept at it, accepting each challenge that came his way in drama school. When he was asked by his acting teacher to play a guy who was badly burned, he blew the room away. The accolades he received from his peers proved yet again that he had nothing to feel guilty about.

"In a way my spirit was coming out; it was a mysterious thing," recalls Martin. There was no stopping him. The recognition he got from his work fuelled a confidence he'd never experienced before. The fellow acting students he roomed with became like the family he'd never had, and their constant praise and positive reinforcement was "incredibly liberating," says Martin. "For the first time, I felt like I belonged."

Martin knew he was different. His new friends had families who sent them money and care packages, while he had to survive by pumping gas. But he started to see his own childhood experiences as a gift. He realized what it was like not to feel guilty, not to feel that there was something wrong with him and those feelings became a trigger for him to take action. This action turned to practice, liberating him to pursue his passion. This practice led to him becoming exceptional at his chosen profession, earning praise from his colleagues. That praise and encouragement helped him build from strength to strength and gave him a glimpse into a successful future.

"I began to realize that what developed in my imagination from childhood was not only acceptable, it was special and rare. I would think it was just a legacy of how I'd lived, but I didn't appreciate what a gift it was until my career was well under way."

Martin has since gone on to play a string of roles in *Victor Victoria, Talk Radio, Star Trek, Dallas, Dangerous Curves*, and *Law & Order*. He's won acclaim as a stage actor at New York's Shakespeare in the Park, the Public Theater, and on Broadway. Most recently, he earned raves for his off-Broadway role as a dying Sigmund Freud in *Freud's Last Session*. He is a working actor, rich in friendships, who has a close relationship with his grown son, who admires his father for "achieving so much with so little."

Today, Martin's freedom burns so brightly that it's enabling him to beat an advanced stage of prostate cancer well past his prognosis—but that's another book! Martin also credits the inner strength he developed as a child on his ability to heal himself both emotionally and physically. All those years of being bent down in guilt and shame as a child taught him to revel in his freedom as an adult to push his limits and try new things. The guilt that caused him an ulcer as a little boy has led to the sense of freedom that is allowing him to beat cancer.

"I feel blessed. Those terrible years were precious to me."

IF SHE CAN BE FREE, SO CAN I

The guilt that children who witness domestic violence feel is so insidious, cropping up in unexpected ways, no matter what their rational minds tell them. Even after they find a greater sense of self-worth and a deeper faith in the purpose of their lives, it can be difficult to shake the feeling that there is something inherently wrong with them or that they could have done more to stop the violence they experienced. Deep down, at key times, it may come back. Just as it did for Martin, until he took action to get out of that pattern. But if you continue to buy into the illusion of guilt, it is hard to act. Why? Guilt is like an addiction that sticks with us and eats away at our self-esteem and willpower. Guilt can cripple you, and become the most subtle source of stress in your life.

Self-expression, or indeed any form of sharing, helps release the guilt. Sharing helps us understand our experience through the eyes of another. Faith, a mother of four from Windsor, Ontario, eventually freed herself of some of her burden through writing her story, which she shared with others as a cautionary tale. But hers is an especially heavy load because, like many who grew up living with domestic violence, her choices as an adult and parent helped perpetuate the cycle.

As far back as she can remember Faith's mother was a source of constant abuse. First, her biological father was on the receiving end of her rants, putting him down with vile insults until he couldn't take it anymore. By the time Faith was five, he left, and her mother used child visitation as a punishment, telling Faith and her younger sister he didn't want them and promising visits from her dad only to cancel them at the last minute. He eventually gave up trying and disappeared from their lives altogether.

Within months of her father's departure, Faith's mother found a new man, a kind of soul mate, if you will, as he was just as much of a hothead as she was. Each night, Faith and her sister would go to bed afraid and to the sound of screaming and wake up the next morning to find projectile objects, like clocks and phones, smashed on the floor. But her mother kept him around. He was a good provider who did her bidding.

"From the outside everything looked fine. We had a nice home, went on great vacations. But inside it was hell."

Faith not only watched all the violence between her parents but was subjected to it as well, as are about half of all children who grow up with domestic violence. But the violence she endured was extreme. Faith, who admits "I had a mouth on me," was singled out in the family. She was subjected to regular beatings by her stepfather while her mother looked on, not only refusing to stop the abuse but encouraging and often ordering him to dole out the punishment.

As she got older, the beatings intensified. And because it fell upon her to do all the housework and childcare, looking after her younger brother and her new half sister, Faith became more defiant and angry. In retaliation, she talked back and stole money. . . and caught hell for it—a cycle of rebellion and retribution that became routine. But the abuse was about to get much worse.

IF SHE CAN SHARE, SO CAN I

Faith's stepfather used to restore antique furniture in the garage that adjoined the house. When she was thirteen, she walked in to get something and stumbled upon a huge hydroponics system for growing marijuana. She started snooping and came across deep freezers filled to the top with the drug. While Faith always knew he was a pothead, constantly rolling and smoking joints around the house, she had no idea he was a big-time drug dealer.

When Faith's stepfather caught her looking, he went berserk, slamming her against the garage wall and threatening to kill her and anyone else she told. "I was petrified," she told her mother. And her mother responded, "Shut up, you are just causing problems." And from that day forward, Faith became an outcast in her own home, a fact highlighted by the much kinder treatment her siblings received. She was barely tolerated because "I was there to work, with no reward or praise for good behavior. I felt like their slave."

Two years later, at fifteen, Faith had finally had enough. It was bedtime and she'd just finished cleaning up the kitchen and was climbing down the stairs to her room when her stepfather yelled at her to get back in the kitchen to resweep the floor. Apparently she'd missed a spot. When Faith snapped back, "Do it yourself," he grabbed her by the hair, dragged her into her room. She tried to call the police, but her mother had disconnected all the phones.

She couldn't take another day in that house. A few friends were aware of her situation, and one of them offered to let her sleep in a camper in the back of his house, which gave her the peace and quiet she craved. But the reprieves were only temporary. After her grade nine graduation, Faith needed a more permanent plan. She'd seen a show on television about teenage mothers, which gave her an idea. Her country's generous welfare system pays single mothers and offers them heavily subsidized housing.

"In my young and naive brain, that was the solution."

So Faith ran away from home to hide out at the home of her boyfriend's family, who welcomed her. Because he went to a different school and wasn't known to her parents, there was less risk of her parents finding out where she was. As far as she knew, her parents didn't even attempt to come looking for her.

But almost immediately after she became pregnant, she discovered that the situation at her boyfriend's house was as chaotic as it had been with her own family. His parents were completely dysfunctional, both addicted to drugs, with several cousins in the extended family cycling in and out of foster care. Still, Faith noticed, "everyone pulled together to help one another out; there was no judgment and they treated me like a part of their family." Her boyfriend's mother was also "the very first person to tell me that she loved me, and mean it." Her boyfriend was a sweet guy who did his best by her, although he was constantly in trouble with the law.

Still just a kid herself at sixteen, Faith moved out, got herself onto financial assistance, found her own place in government-funded housing, and enrolled in a school for pregnant teens. Unfazed by the idea of looking after a baby, having single-handedly raised her younger siblings, she was looking forward to the unconditional love of her own child and determined to make a better life for herself. "For the first time in my life," she says, "I felt in control of the situation; I had managed to somehow balance the dysfunction."

WHY SHOULD SHE FEEL GUILTY?

Still, Faith felt guilty. Seeing how other families were together, even how her own siblings were treated in comparison with her, Faith always wondered if she somehow deserved to be the target of her parents' anger. On some level, she thought the violence must somehow be her fault. She recalls thinking, "If I'd been more obedient or complained less about missing my birth father or hadn't discovered all those drugs in the garage, my parents might have treated me better."

As a young adult or adult reading this, you see how illogical this is, don't you? Perhaps some of your beliefs concerning what you are falsely guilty about are equally as illogical. A child's brain finds evidence, false reasons, to confirm guilt. Children can't see that they're blameless, that they are not responsible for the actions of adults who should be protecting, not injuring, them. They can't see that they are inherently good. Instead, they feel they've failed and are left feeling profoundly sad and regretful, even as adults. Can you fathom how it must feel to consider yourself at fault for not preventing one parent from hurting another?

Even those who were obviously not guilty can believe this lie. It's a common theme. As clinical psychologist Richard McNally explains, although a person who suffered as a child may find it difficult to recall details from each particular occurrence, they will never forget what it *felt* like.[3] So as an adult we remember the feelings of guilt and shame quite well, but we don't recall all the details and really don't want to bring up all of those memories again, leaving us to go on believing the lie as adults.

Faith was still in the cycle, trapped in that lie of guilt. When she moved out of her boyfriend's family home it seemed at first as if she were on her way. She was doing well in school and staying focused. But she was still a teenage mother living on her own who craved love and acceptance. She was isolated and vulnerable, and that made her a walking target. By nineteen, seeing all her peers get married and have babies, she was feeling lonely. She met a guy at a keg party who said all the right things. He was four years older, employed, and instantly told her she was meant to be with him forever. He promised marriage, more babies, and protection from her estranged family.

I DID THE UNTHINKABLE

But almost immediately the violence started. And within three weeks of meeting him, she was pregnant. "He was basically my stepfather," admits Faith. "And although we never married, I stayed with him for the next four years, and had two more children by him. I know now that I thought I didn't deserve better. I'd convinced myself that no other man would want me. He never hugged me; he never told me he loved me. It was basically the same relationship I had with my mother."

Even though her own children were now growing up with domestic violence, she thought that she was protecting her kids because they were not being physically abused. But we know that the psychological impact is just as damaging. An astonishing nine out of ten parents believe that either their kids don't know or it won't affect them, but nine out of ten children *do* know, and there is plenty of evidence to confirm that the impact is profound. It reached the point at which Faith could no longer deny this truth: "The last thing I wanted was to repeat the cycle with my kids."

She finally reached her limit when the violence escalated to a level at which she truly feared for her life. It took almost dying to set Faith free.

"Lying there, with his hands around my neck, I started to think of everything I had to live for, all the things that, at twenty-two, I still wanted to do, and an amazing feeling went through my whole body, a sense of knowing that I would be OK."

"Still, I remember my seven-year-old punching him with his little fists and crying. I wished I could make this all go away—my son should never have to defend me." It was just one more layer of guilt for Faith.

Sometimes you have to reach your breaking point before you let yourself be free. Faith was already there.

"I knew I had to show my kids that this was not acceptable, and the only way to do that was to never let this happen again," she says. She had to be the One for her kids.

And finally she moved, changed her number, and enrolled in college to get her nursing degree. Other than contact over care of the kids and attempts at co-parenting, Faith stopped calling him and gained sole custody of the children.

As psychologist Sonja Lyubomirsky explains, action is critical: "The next step after acknowledging regrets is to move on by committing ourselves to new pursuits."[4]

For the first time in years, Faith built up a social network outside the home. By befriending and mentoring other women who'd shared similar stories and by opening up about her own life, she realized she was not alone. It all helped her shed some of that shame she'd been carrying with her for so long.

Faith was discovering what it was like to feel truly free. Within the year she was earning a comfortable living running a day surgery unit in a hospital, and through that accomplishment, she gained self-confidence. She slowly started to date again, although she was cautious about letting any new men into her life.

When she was twenty-seven, she met Gregory: a gentleman who was patient, loving, and kind. She waited six months before introducing him to her kids. She gradually allowed herself to be loved. They married and moved into a nice home in a safe, middle-class neighborhood on the other side of town.

Now, when those old lies creep back into Faith's consciousness and the guilt weighs her down, she knows what actions to take: "I have to talk about it; I have to get it out. It makes me feel so much better."

To that end, Faith began journaling. And when she heard about CDV on the *Dr. Phil* show, she decided to share her story on the CDV website. "It was scary to tell it, and weird, but it felt so good," she says. "It's one of the best things I have done since all this happened."

WHY TAKING ACTION AND SHARING ARE KEYS TO FREEDOM

Faith figured out something that the experts have known for years. As Lyubomirsky reminds us, "Putting our emotional upheavals into words helps us to make sense of them, accommodate them, and begin to move past them. It ultimately prepares us to share these upheavals with close others."[5]

Psychologist and trauma expert William Stiles says the desire to talk after going through situations of distress is a natural and healthy impulse, and the mind's way of healing itself, "like a fever after an infection."[6] Talking through experiences with others allows us to convert upsetting, traumatic experiences into forms of post-traumatic growth. In his book, *What Doesn't Kill Us: The New Psychology of Post-Traumatic Growth*, Stephen Joseph likens the process of talking it out to our hands shaping a piece of modeling clay. In the same way, our words help shape the meaning that we make of an experience.[7]

Sharing our stories exposes the false logic behind the lie. It reveals all the erroneous, unquestioned assumptions that children make. As brain expert David Sousa explains, "These children are also drawing false conclusions . . . they think that their mere presence at the scene of violence somehow makes them responsible. They say to themselves: *It only happens when I'm around, so I must be the problem, I must somehow be to blame.*"

STAYING AWAKE SO I COULD TAKE ACTION

Guilt and shame are things I've always struggled with. I felt responsible. It was my fault, I should have stopped it. I felt great shame because I believed there was something wrong with me. I was no good. I wondered if I was the only one who felt this scared. I was weak. But I couldn't bear to admit any of it. I would do anything to avoid blame, to the point of trying to prove that others were wrong, be it a waiter in a restaurant or a colleague at work. And today I can see that it all traces back to what happened when I was just a skinny little kid trying to stop two grown adults from hurting one another.

I was certain that it was my fault that my mother got hit. On nights when Keith came over, I made it my job to creep out of bed to listen and sometimes wait from the top of the stairs as they argued, gripping the spindles tightly. I never quite knew how bad it was going to get.

From the top of the stairs I would watch. There was always a moment, like a calm before the storm, when Keith would back away and stop talking, because he'd finally had enough. His fingers would start twitching, hitting the soft part of the palm, making a sound like someone just learning to snap. That was my cue.

I would sprint downstairs and put myself between the two of them. Sometimes it worked and my unexpected appearance created just enough of a distraction to stop their fight. But on other nights, I just got pushed out of the way—hard. I'd bang my head against the wall and be lying on the ground. He would turn away for a moment as if he were trying to stop himself and then suddenly swing his hand into her face. It always got worse from there. I got hit only as an afterthought or if my mother snapped at me.

Whenever my mother got hit, I felt the blow inside me. It was like a knife being jabbed into my stomach. Like so many children of domestic violence, I wished that I could have been the target instead of being a helpless witness. It hurt me so much to see her struck, and I blamed myself every time, because I hadn't come down in time or I wasn't strong enough to stop it. I could invent any number of reasons; I was utterly convinced that it was my sole responsibility, even as a small child, to defend her against this enormous man

SHARING WITH A STRANGER

It was something I never discussed with anyone until well into adulthood, when I shared what happened in a random conversation with a stranger. I don't know why I chose to share. Perhaps I was guided to do so. Perhaps I was at such a low point that it couldn't get any worse. Whatever the reason, it was one of the best decisions I ever made in my life, because it was only after I shared that I was able to launch into action.

"I let it go on for all these years, even though I had the opportunity to stop it," I told the stranger. "Because of that I lack confidence. I wonder how a man could let that happen. I let the fear inside stop me."

The fact was I hated myself for not acting, not realizing at the time that guilt destroys your willpower to act. Sharing what I viewed to be a terrible weakness, I felt ashamed. But the guy looked at me like I had two heads and said: "What do you mean? You were six years old! I can't imagine the courage it took to live through that."

The moment I heard that, I can't say I fully believed it, like a compliment you don't accept, but I did begin to find more and more evidence as to why that statement was true. That conversation came flooding back to me when I heard our experts discuss guilt as one of the ten lies.

Sandra Graham-Bermann, professor of psychology at the University of Michigan, founded Kids' Club, a prevention and intervention program for children coming from violent homes. Through her work, she discovered that speaking and hearing the truth that they are not in any way responsible for the fighting between their parents can be transformational to these children. Their entire demeanor changes after they hear that truth.

"It's like a mantra—we have them chant it out, sing it out, draw it out," says Graham-Bermann. "We put a lot of energy into that message, and when they hear it you can see them grinning from ear to ear."

Who knows the impact on my life if I'd heard those words earlier? But how could I? We never discussed; we never shared; no one ever talked about it. It was taboo. But the fact is I did finally hear them, and now I understand. I've accepted the core truth that it's never the fault of a child when their parents fight. There was nothing we could have done differently that would have led to a different outcome.

SHARING HER STORY SETS MY MOTHER FREE

A few years ago, I asked my mother if she would talk to a researcher who was helping me with this book. After much discussion, she reluctantly agreed.

I listened to the recording of the interview with some preconceived notion of what I'd hear, never expecting the revelations to come.

After the initial pleasantries, the interviewer asked my mother, "If you were to use one word to summarize your childhood what would it be?"

"Violent," she said.

Frustrated, I said to myself, "No, Mom, he said *your* childhood, not mine!"

As the interview continued, I listened in amazement. It was as if *I* were the one answering the questions. She had experienced the same things I did—some worse, some not as bad.

It never even occurred to me that she could have experienced the same thing I did. I learned so much in that conversation, I had to stop the tape a few times, to cry. I felt so bad, as though she were my child, not the other way around. I wanted to take away the pain.

She described how my grandmother and grandfather and Keith had all experienced the same thing, which I would later learn is common.

At the end of that conversation for the first time I felt liberated. Why? Because the truth was so clear: She was repeating a pattern that was instilled in her. She did not have the knowledge to break out of it.

I couldn't believe that I didn't ask her about her own childhood experiences so much earlier. I simply never knew to ask. I never knew this was so critical.

FREEDOM IS MADE VISIBLE THROUGH ACTION

As McGonigal reminds us, guilt, like other forms of stress, is "the enemy of willpower."[8] Guilt makes it almost impossible to act with any consistency. But now that you are free from the guilt you can take steps toward fulfilling your potential.

All it takes is action. As mentioned at the beginning of this chapter, freedom can be made visible through action. When you were young, this was second nature. You were conditioned to take action when you needed to most, even if that action was simply to find a safe place.

Think of all those actions you took to protect not only yourself but your younger sibling, mother, or father. I spent most of my childhood sitting at the top of the staircase watching, deciding whether I should act or hide. Yet I spent most of my adult life beating myself up for not taking it further, when I was already doing more than any child should.

Over these next pages, you'll meet others who took action as children, like Olivia, who would run to the phone to call 911 over and over again, or Chelsea, who, when her parents were arguing at night, made a tent out of a baton and blanket and sang songs to her little brothers and sisters to distract them and make them feel safe. These are actions no seven-year-old should have to take, much less think about, and yet she did.

Remember those many times as a child when you did the same, when you acted instinctively. Even inaction was action because it was the smart decision that kept you safe. Maybe it crushes you inside because you felt you should have done more. No, you did exactly what you should have, because putting yourself in harm's way could have made it worse for everybody. Maybe you look back on those moments you acted decisively, beyond your years, and you still think to yourself, "But I had no choice." Yes, you did. Those were actions you did not have to take, but you chose to do things that took courage and strength at a time when you should have been sleeping safely in your own bed. Even if that action was to hide, you showed resolve. You did something. Keeping yourself out of harm's way took a strength and awareness that was beyond your years.

For most adults, willpower is about knowing you have to do push-ups and eat healthier to lose some weight. That doesn't even compare to what you had to face as a child. Somehow, you had to find the resolve to survive at a time when you should have been protected and nurtured instead. More than anyone, you were conditioned to take action. But since then you've learned a lie that's held you back. Remember, guilt makes it almost impossible to act with any consistency.

Now that you are free from the guilt and shame, you can rediscover that willpower you had as a child and take those necessary steps toward fulfilling your dreams—whatever they may be.

These can be small and simple actions, such as putting your thoughts and experiences into words. This tool comes from trauma expert James Pennebaker's groundbreaking "writing paradigm," in which expressive writing helps bring understanding and perspective to traumatic experiences. It's just enough of a time commitment to have an impact without being overwhelming, and it works.

These steps will lead to greater actions that will help get you closer to reaching your full potential. How? You are freeing yourself from the very things that have been holding you back—guilt and shame—and that freedom is made visible through action. From now on, you'll be able to move forward, because nothing is holding you back from making and acting on the choices that lead you closer to your full potential.

By working through our false shame and exposing the false sense of guilt that hides behind it, we can learn to see the past through a different filter and free ourselves to act, and act consistently.

Remember, children think emotionally, not rationally. When you experienced domestic violence as a child, your brain drew the wrong conclusions: "I couldn't stop it, but I should have. I was there, so it must have been my fault. There must be something wrong with me. It happened because of me." But now, as an adult, you know that violence between parents is never a child's fault.

Your adult brain is now developed and you understand this rationally. But have you truly allowed yourself to feel this truth emotionally? Whether it's writing in a journal or simply having a dialogue with a stranger, unpack the baggage of self-blame by sharing your story with someone else. Rediscover your past through their eyes. This works, because conversation helps transform the meaning. It was never your fault, so now it's time to allow yourself to really feel that way.

Today you are free from that environment. You have taken that first critical step toward freedom because you are aware of the truth. You know what you were never told, that a child can never be held responsible for the actions of an adult, ever. Your adult brain needs to hear that! When you were young your child brain wrongfully concluded that you were at fault, that you should have stopped it, and sadly, your adult brain that controls rational thinking was not formed to help you see the truth.

Now as an adult, it is so much a part of you, that you don't even question it. But question it you must because you know it is a lie. As an adult today, would you look at a young child and think that he or she was truly responsible for your actions? Of course not! As of this moment, you are free from the illusion of guilt and shame that has held you back from reaching your true potential—free from the lie.

FROM THE LIE TO THE TRUTH

The Lie

You are somehow responsible for the violence you lived with during early life. It was somehow your fault or you could have stopped it.

The Why

As a child the emotional brain is fully developed, but the neocortex, the logical thinking center, is not fully developed until adulthood. As a child you felt all the emotion fully but you did not have a developed, rationale part of the brain to understand what was happening—to understand the truth. Thus as a child, you falsely concluded that it was your fault or that you could have done something differently to alter the outcome. This belief then becomes part of you and becomes true and is not challenged in adulthood. It is simply fact.

The Truth

I am free. I am free from the environment of my childhood. It is now my time to be free from the illusion of guilt and shame.

I embody this freedom, this truth and act as such, by remembering that taking action is a skill I worked to develop early in my life. I use that skill to my benefit, and I act when others do not.

Freedom is not something I can physically see. But freedom gives me the choice to take action. So my freedom is made visible through action. I now know that guilt and shame destroy willpower and this false belief has held me back long enough.

I act in ways that move me closer to my full potential.

To Try

You have already taken the first step toward who you were meant to be. And how did you take that step? You acted. You took action by picking up this book and reading it. Reinforce this truth by taking some or all of the following actions.

1. Throughout the day if a thought triggers a feeling of guilt or shame, or if you have a desire to blame something on another, pause and breathe deeply and remember this important truth: A child is never responsible for causing or stopping the actions of adults.

2. Share. But before sharing with another, share with yourself. Once we understand what happened we can be fully free.

3. For the next four days, spend fifteen minutes each day in a quiet place and write out what you would share with someone. You can write whatever you wish. No one else will read it, so don't worry about grammar or making it sound perfect. The secret is just to write. Here are a few questions and actions to help you along.

- What was your childhood like?
- What memories trouble you the most?
- What did you believe about yourself because of these memories?
- Now, as you look back, would you conclude the same about another child in that position? Was he or she really guilty? Could he or she really stop it? Was it truly that child's fault? Was there something wrong with that child?
- So what is the truth?
- With this truth in mind, what does your life look like?
- What do you want to have happen this year?

3

RESENTFUL TO COMPASSIONATE

Resentment is like drinking poison and hoping it will kill your enemies.　　　　　　　　　　　—Nelson Mandela

The lies we learn as we grow up living with domestic violence are all connected. When guilt and shame get buried deep within ourselves they create a self-hatred—we don't like who we have become. Our childhood belief that "it was my fault," "there was something with me" so therefore "I don't deserve any better" translates into a lack of compassion for ourselves, which in turn becomes resentment. If we can't feel compassion for ourselves, how can we feel it for others? We think, "Bad things happened to me, so why would I want good things to happen to someone else." And when deep down you want bad things to happen to others, how can you be a good person?

Resentment is part of this toxic cycle; we get stuck. It's self-blame turned outward, which gets unleashed onto the rest of the world. With that mind-set, we go through life expecting the worst from others and seeking out the signs. In fact, we've become so good at it, we'd make great detectives. It's as if we had a sixth sense, or intuition, about when something bad is about to go down.

It's a kind of street smarts we developed as children growing up in these homes in order to survive. Psychological and physical street smarts. As child psychologist Bruce Perry points out in *The Boy Who Was Raised As a Dog*, the traumatized child has already experienced more selective development of "nonverbal cognitive capacities."[1] He or she has learned that "non-verbal communication is more important than verbal." We learned how to read every gesture, facial expression, each nonverbal cue to prepare ourselves for the next wave of violence. We had to.

But here's the good news. That intuition is a gift. It's the tool that can lead to a heightened awareness about others that becomes compassion. Instead of finding reasons to resent those who may have had it easier, our ability to read the bad signs can just as easily be used to find the good in others. When resentment triggers, we can step back, ask a question, and use our street smarts to better understand a situation. As Marina discovered, perceptiveness was the secret weapon that, when used correctly, allowed her to get out of her own head and arrive at a completely different emotional state, where her heart could swell with empathy and compassion. Instead of living under a cloud of bitterness, she was finally able to experience joy.

WHY WOULD A PARENT RESENT THEIR CHILD FOR HAVING IT BETTER THEN THEM?

The first few years of Marina's life in rural Argentina were in many ways ideal. Her early childhood was full of laughter, family feasts, warmth, and security. Her mother, grandparents, uncles, aunts, and cousins played together, ate together, protected each other, and cherished the presence of this bright-eyed, inquisitive little girl. They taught her everything she needed to know about familial love. They were so close, she even shared a bed with her grandmother, who, along with a beloved uncle, helped raise her while her mother was away at work.

Marina's dad, Raoul, had left just months after she was born to seek his fortune in America. When her parents met they hadn't known each other for long, and Marina wasn't planned. They got married because "in a small town in Latin America that's what you did when you got pregnant," but her dad decided it was best to try his luck in the land of dreams. His own family was poor and uneducated, so he was determined to prove his worth and show everyone that he was somebody to be reckoned with.

By the time Marina turned six, her mother wrote to her father and asked for a divorce. It seemed obvious he was never going to be a part of the family picture back in Argentina, so it was time to make that official. But Marina's dad pleaded with her mother to come to the United States and bring Marina. He told her he was ready to provide a comfortable life for his wife and daughter, and wanted to try to be a family. Marina's mom figured it would be unfair to her daughter if she didn't give her a chance to get to know her birth father, so she agreed.

"She didn't want to have me grow up without a father and have me ask about him later in life," Marina explains. "She didn't want me to live without that experience and regret it later."

By then Marina's mom didn't feel much for the man, but at least, she thought, he was trying to do the right thing by his family. An education in America for their daughter would be an added bonus. Marina's father had fulfilled his ambition and become a success, establishing a thriving catering business in the Northeast. It should have been a fresh start filled with promise. Instead, it was the beginning of a joyless upbringing full of emotional abuse that bred sadness, bitterness, and resentment.

Marina's dad was a child of domestic violence. But as an adult, he wasn't physically violent toward his family. He prided himself on never laying a hand on them, and reminded them of this fact often, as if Marina and her mother should consider themselves lucky they weren't being hit. But his words and other actions were purposely chosen to cause pain in another way. Although he considered himself superior to his own father because he wasn't physically abusive, the put-downs and reprimands were as constant as they were harsh. It was as if he resented his wife and daughter for having a "better life" than he had experienced.

As Rick Warren explains, many people are driven by resentment. They hold on to their hurt and never get over it. Instead of releasing their pain through forgiveness, they rehearse it over and over again in their minds. But releasing your resentment and revealing your feeling is the first step to healing.[2]

At mealtimes, Raoul refused to sit down with his wife and daughter and barely interacted with them at home unless it was to find fault with something. They never took vacations together. He never joined in on family gatherings. He was territorial, isolating them from friends in order to "protect" them—at least that was his rationale if ever he bothered to explain his actions. And he was stingy, refusing to give Marina lunch money for school if her mother was away at work. Marina, who was young and not yet able to speak the language fluently, felt isolated in unfamiliar surroundings and was forced to find her own way.

"I would walk home from school in the pouring rain countless times," she remembers, "because he refused to pick me up."

ONLY THOSE WHO HAVE SUFFERED CAN TRULY UNDERSTAND SUFFERING

The emotional deep freeze was beyond hurtful to Marina. But her father's neglect was nowhere near as difficult as the sting of watching him put down her mother. In front of Marina and other people, he would call her a "stupid bitch" and every other foul name he could think of. Marina doesn't recall any physical violence toward her or her mother. It was nonphysical violence, which is equally damaging.

By the time Marina turned fourteen, the family had moved back to Argentina. Marina's mother thought the change of environment would do her husband good. It would also give Marina back some of the support system from her grandmother, aunts, and uncles. But nothing got better among father, mother, and daughter. In fact, it grew worse.

"The problem was within him," recalls Marina. "In his mind, no one had compassion for him; no one wanted to alleviate his suffering, so he had no compassion for himself or others, no empathy himself. He was not aware."

As anthropologist Sarah Blaffer Hrdy explains, one of the things we know about empathy is that the potential is expressed only under certain rearing conditions.[3]

Over the next three years, the anger and resentment escalated. Marina started standing up for herself and defending her mother. Her dad's hostility became unrelenting. Communication took the form of yelling and slamming doors. Although he never hit them, he punched walls and doors, as if to say, "I'm not hitting you, but I could if I wanted to."

The worst of it would happen when her mother wasn't at home.

Typically, he would push Marina's buttons in the hope of starting an argument, which usually ended up in a screaming match. The emotional and verbal violence reached a boiling point when she was eighteen. Father and daughter had gotten into yet another argument, during which he called her mother a slut—and Marina completely lost it.

A scuffle ensued, which ended up with her father's hands around her neck, almost choking her to death. Marina is tiny, about five foot one, and her father was a big man, over six feet tall, yet she somehow managed to free herself from his grip. Then she grabbed the car keys from the kitchen table and ran out, seeking safety with some relatives. The rest was a blur. Her entire body was in pain from the struggle so she took too much pain medication and somehow ended up in the ER, with her father's handprints still on her neck.

That was it. That fight was, she said, "the culminating moment of all those years of anger and resentment I felt toward him." She immediately moved in with her aunt, and her mother, who now had a pathway to get out of the marriage, followed her daughter a few weeks after. Marina has not spoken to her father since.

HER BITTERNESS LINGERS INTO ADULTHOOD

Back with the family she knew as a little girl, life got better. Once again, she was in an environment of peace, love, and acceptance. But inside, she felt anything but calm and secure. In fact, she was seething. For the next few years, all she felt was a slow-burning anger toward her father.

"Anytime that scene [of the last violent encounter] replayed in my mind I felt a complete and total lack of control. I was sad and resentful, and I felt those lies even more after I distanced myself from him. All I could think about was the fact that the person who was supposed to care for me and love me the most was doing these things."

As a result, Marina closed herself off from loving relationships, never quite able to live fully in the moment and quick to react when she sensed someone was about to do her wrong—particularly boyfriends. She consistently picked men who were like her father and became furious with them each time they behaved remotely like him.

Resentment is a buried rage. It's a bitterness that never seems to go away. Marina's father suffered from this, and succumbed. His behavior demonstrated that when you are trapped in that lie, you may feel little to no compassion for others. You don't want to help them because no one helped you. It's why you have no compassion for yourself. Maybe you don't want something good to happen to someone else. Perhaps you plot the deaths of those who harmed you. Maybe it's hardened you into thinking, "I want what I want, and I don't care about the needs of others."

As Sonja Lyubomirsky explains, feeling "personally deflated as a result of other people's successes, accomplishments, and triumphs and feeling relieved rather that sympathetic in the face of other people's failures and undoings is a poor prescription for happiness."[4]

However this resentment manifests, it can linger and fester like a cancer, draining all the color and joy out of life. It's a toxic emotion that keeps you from moving forward. You can't release the past, so you're stuck in it. And that's why resentment is bottled up *old* anger, an effort to relive a past hurt.

Unlike anger, there is no outward expression of emotion with resentment. When you are in a state of resentment you typically hold it in, fuming and embittered, consumed by grievances. It's all about hostility, blame, and all-consuming envy. While anger often results in aggressive behavior in reaction to a perceived threat, resentment is felt after the injury has already occurred. It is not expressed as aggressively or as openly. Anger is an emotion you feel in the moment—whereas resentment is the *accumulation* of anger that has gone *unexpressed*. But, as Warren puts it, "Those who have hurt you in your past cannot continue to hurt you now, unless you hold on to the pain through resentment."[5]

Resentment is a persistent part of the lie that many children of domestic violence internalize from their difficult experiences. Marina and her father are not exceptions. They hang on to their pain like an unpaid debt, and they try to tear others down—whether openly or in their minds—in the futile hope that it will satisfy them somehow. Marina couldn't feel joy in others and was constantly finding fault, a reason to push people away. The lie is that they believe they will feel better by making others feel worse; it's payback for the past. Instead, every harsh word said, cold shoulder given, and praise withheld turns on you, and you end up resenting yourself more each day. You tell yourself no one had compassion for you, so how can you have it for yourself, let alone for another?

The truth is that only through awareness can those who grew up living with domestic violence find the resolution they seek. Compassion is the only payback that will heal and lift them up, because they need to first have self-compassion before they can have it for another. And this comes through awareness. When they start to comprehend what happened, not only through their own eyes but from the perspective of others, this understanding is the first step in taking them from resentment to compassion.

THE ONE FOR MARINA HELPS HER FORGIVE HERSELF

Marina had a boyfriend who, in her words, "had hints of my father," and she took much of her resentment out on him. She was often skittish and hotheaded, snapping easily. She lived in her head, putting walls up even to those to whom she was closest. She came to realize that she didn't trust men, believing that if she was attracted to them there must be something wrong. She didn't want to open up to anyone or make herself vulnerable because she saw where that landed her mother.

Marina's aunt, a nurse with some experience in family counseling, recognized that her niece's behavior would lead only to lifelong unhappiness as long as she was unaware of why she acted the way she did. And, for Marina, her aunt became the One.

"This is not your fault," she told her niece. "What happened is no reflection on you."

When Marina asked what she meant, she says that her aunt told that, although part of her still believed she had done something wrong, Marina was the child. She should have been taken care of and protected. The rest was not her responsibility. But if she held on to that anger, fear, and sadness toward her father, it would eat away at her.

Marina's aunt was helping her see the truth that, in Rick Warren's words, "those who have hurt you in your past cannot continue to hurt you now, unless you hold on to the pain through resentment."[6]

This conversation opened the door for Marina to think about forgiveness in a different way: not to forgive for another, but to forgive *for herself*. It may have been too difficult at the moment for her to forgive her father fully. But as Marina discovered, not forgiving was simply causing her more pain in the form of resentment. She decided that resentment would not be the defining factor in her life. Marina does not condone her father's actions— or her own. Forgiveness does not excuse. It simply allows you to say (or simply picture yourself saying), "I forgive you for not being the parent I wish you could have been because I understand you were doing the best you could with what you knew." This process of forgiveness could begin with asking your parents, What was your childhood like? It is among the most powerful questions you can ever ask because it will lead you to an awareness and understanding beyond anything you could imagine. It is the first step toward empathy that will lead to true forgiveness.

Marina often tells herself, "I am not Marina who resents that her childhood was taken away; I am Marina who is smart, funny, friendly, and whom people like being around." She remembers her true characteristics. She thinks back to that bright-eyed, loving and beloved little girl who cuddled with her grandmother at night. She feels compassion for that child—and this is the key element. If you don't have compassion for yourself—a desire to take away the pain from one who has suffered—how can you have it for another?

Only those who have suffered can truly understand suffering. Marina realized her suffering was a gift, although not one she would have wished for, but a gift nevertheless. With this realization, she started to live the life she was supposed to lead. She graduated from college and moved to Boston to start a career with an exciting young start-up working with some of the biggest advertisers in the world. Today, when she meets people, she's open, and not so quick to judge. Fortunately, she'd had enough of a foundation from her early years to remember what it was like to feel happy and loved. When she thinks about it, she knows she is capable of having that feeling again. But first, she had to let go of her resentment.

"Suddenly I realized I had been hurting myself more by being so resentful and directing my anger at this person," she admits. "It was not my fault. There was nothing I could do about it but to try to grow and heal and make a life that was different."

Marina now understands that resentment "festers in you and then you direct it at other people who had nothing to do with what happened." When she thinks about her father, it is no longer with anger. Instead, she feels compassion for him. The domestic violence her father lived with was a constant theme in his life and something he never got over. She forgave him for doing the very best with what he knew.

Perhaps if he had been able to share or had the fortune of having someone who was compassionate toward him, it would have been different. Marina could still be that person missing from her father's life. It is never too late to tell someone who wronged you, "I forgive you for not being everything I hoped you would be, and I am sorry that you were hurt when you were a child."

Marina was able to get out of her own head and feel compassion for her father, who was trapped in his own endless state of resentment. In doing so, she developed compassion for herself. As I discussed at the beginning of this chapter, growing up with domestic violence gives you this secret skill: an uncanny ability to perceive what is going on with others—you have a remarkable intuition.

This is not just some blanket statement; it is scientific fact. Developmental neurobiologist R. Douglas Fields, author of *The Other Brain*, says that, according to recent neuroimaging research, abuse and neglect produce long-lasting changes in the connections between the left and right brain, the amygdala, and the prefrontal cortex.[7] One aspect of this change means that the brain is "trained" to constantly monitor the environment for danger. Of course, that's not entirely a positive. This instinct takes over the conscious mind, resulting in lower thresholds for rage. The altered brain circuitry can also predispose women to more mood and anxiety disorders.[8] But that heightened ability to detect a threat is real. The brain is a highly adaptive and plastic organ. Your amygdala detects threats in the environment, so that you can respond quickly. Your hippocampus maps out the environment, forms memories of events, and learns the context of when experiences, like threats and stresses, are likely to be experienced, says Fields.

In other words, you developed this skill from a very early age because you had to read body language and understand nonverbal communication to figure out what the night would bring. You developed this over years, and it's caused you pain. But, leveraged the right way, intuition can become a pathway toward compassion.

COMPASSION CAN SAVE YOUR LIFE

When you discover the power of compassion, kindness, and empathy, it really is like a physical weight has lifted. Turning resentment into compassion isn't just a balm for your emotional health; it's something that could *save your life*. Psychologist Carsten Wrosch cites a growing body of research indicating that "persistent bitterness may result in global feelings of anger and hostility that, when strong enough, could affect a person's physical health."[9]

A 2001 study revealed the correlation between *replaying hurtful memories* and the human stress response. Subjects who were encouraged to just *think* compassionate thoughts, experienced lower heart rates and decreased blood pressure. Compassion fostered better anger management skills, lower risk of alcohol or substance abuse, fewer depression and anxiety symptoms, reduction of chronic physical pain, healthier friendships, and greater spiritual well-being.

Beyond the obvious fact that resentment interferes with the experience of pleasure, the body's automatic stress response to resentment contributes directly to high blood pressure and heart disease, and weakens the immune system. We can experience muscle tension, body pain, ulcers, rapid breathing, accelerated heart, headaches, stomach problems, exhaustion, and most notably, heart disease. Studies show chronically hostile or resentful adults with no history of heart trouble are 19 percent more likely than their peers to develop heart disease. And they run triple the risk of having a heart attack or dying over the next five to ten years. Why? Because inside, you are seething, distracted by your grudges, plotting revenge. You want to even the score and punish those who hurt you. So instead of letting go of the past, you stay attached to it, obsessed with the offense.

And that's the burden of resentment: It's an emotion that holds you in its grip and paralyzes you. In the words of the late Nelson Mandela, a man who lived much of his life in unjust captivity, "Resentment is like drinking poison and hoping it will kill your enemies."[10]

Janine knows the bitter taste of resentment all too well. She grew up in an affluent neighborhood just outside Houston and, by all appearances to her neighbors; Janine had a wonderful child-hood, raised in a warm, loving, tight-knit family. Her father was a successful cardiac surgeon and took the family skiing most winter weekends. In the summer, she played with her younger sisters and friends in their backyard pool. She learned how to ride horses and took private tennis lessons at the local racquet club. Her bedroom was filled with toys and posters.

WHY MUST TRAGEDY STRIKE IN ORDER FOR OUR COMPASSIONATE NATURE TO REVEAL ITSELF?

But Janine, the oldest daughter, remembers things a little differ-ently. Her parents often fought after putting the children to bed. From her bedroom she could hear them yelling loudly downstairs. One time she heard her own name and began to worry that she was the cause of their arguments. Some mornings, she would find her father sleeping alone on the couch.

One evening, as her eighth birthday approached, she remem-bers lying in bed thinking excitedly about the upcoming party her mother had planned. Three of her closest friends were going to spend the night and go riding horses at a nearby ranch the next morning. She heard the door open and saw her father's silhouette quietly enter the room, locking the door behind him. He began kissing and touching her.

Then it happened every night for the next five years. Janine held on to her secret for years; just like the fights between her parents, she had convinced herself that it was her fault. Only when she turned fourteen did she dare to reveal to her mother what happened. By that time, her parents had separated and were in the midst of a divorce.

Relocating to New Mexico and leaving her father behind, the family suffered a steep drop in their living standard as their father contested any kind of financial settlement. While her mother tried to find work, Janine struggled with her feelings. She deeply resented all the pain her father had caused her, as well as her mother for breaking up the family.

"I did everything I could to escape my reality. I was hanging out with the wrong crowd and started using a lot of drugs—and drinking too. I couldn't get past what had happened with my parents' divorce. I was very self-centered at that time, and to me it felt like my whole life had fallen apart—the smaller apartment, no more backyard pools, and no more horses. I was so angry but I didn't know who to blame." Blame took away all of her power, even numbing her to the compassion that she should have had for herself.

She remembers those years regretfully. She often picked fights with her sisters and her mother. She began deliberately hurting herself, carving small cuts into her wrists with a razor in her bedroom at night. Although she reluctantly entered counseling at her mother's suggestion, and she stopped the self-mutilation, she remained intensely bitter throughout high school and college, struggling with her feelings of resentment. She developed an aggressive, highly competitive attitude in her studies, which allowed her to get excellent grades, but alienated her from friends.

"I was basically a spiteful person, always holding on to something—that hurt feeling from my past. I remember feeling like people were always trying to take advantage of me. I had a couple close friends, a few boyfriends, but I never really trusted anyone."

Janine would never get physically aggressive. Studies have found that though men and women report they feel anger for an equal number of minutes per day, men get physically aggressive twenty times more often than women do.[11] But inside, she seethed: "People didn't like me that much. I was too prickly. I'd always find a reason to be angry about something, and every time something bad happened to me, it would be further proof that I was right. I was basically allowing my bitterness to define the path of my life."

When Janine's mother was diagnosed with ovarian cancer, everything changed.

Seeing her mother suffer forced Janine to tap into her true nature. Taking care of her mother taught her how to empathize and, eventually, to forgive.

Again, those powers of perception fostered by resentment equipped her to become more aware of her mother's needs. Learning what medicines her mother had to take, reading the signs of the aftereffects of radiation and chemo, gave her a deep understanding of what her mother was going through. Janine put her perceptive nature to work to help another person; she was there every step of the way to relieve her mother's suffering, and that helped her to achieve resentment's opposite: compassion.

The surgery and treatment were successful, and Janine's mother remains in remission, but as is often the case when faced with the possibility of the death of someone we believe has wronged us, we are able to fully embrace the truth. But we don't have to wait for moments like these. Fortunately, Janine was able to feel *compassion* for her mother, and for herself, before it was too late.

"It gave me the wisdom to start seeing beyond my own problems, and my own worries," she says. "I realized that my time with the people I care about is really short, and I can't keep holding on to something that happened so long ago. You can't really live in two places at once, the past and the present, and I just decided that I wanted to focus on what's happening right now."

BILL CLINTON'S SECRET WEAPON

When we believe that someone is trying to hurt us—and we want to hurt them back—the only action that will lead to happiness is to develop compassion for them. By choosing this path not only do we defuse a potentially destructive situation but we enhance our self-esteem. We can't control whether someone is going to try to hurt us, but we can choose to control how we interpret his or her actions and therefore become impervious to the emotional pain.

In his memoir, President Bill Clinton told of his experience growing up with domestic violence. As a young man he was bitter about the position he was put in. He resented others who had peace in their homes. He did not want good things to happen for them. Or at least that was the case until his grandmother told him, "Always want good things for other people. Because if you don't, it won't be possible for you to have anything good happen to you. The more you want bad for others, the more bad happens to you. The more you want and let them know that you want the best for them, the more good happens to you."[12]

As we've learned, the brain finds evidence for what it believes. Clinton believed what his grandmother told him and, with the help of his grandmother's wisdom, was able to move beyond resentment. But he had the experience of being on the receiving end of the emotional pain of domestic violence and that enabled him to develop empathy. Again, he was putting that hidden gift of resentment—the power of perception—to good use. "I feel your pain," he would often say on the campaign trail, and people believed him because it was heartfelt. Like his politics or not, he is viewed as one of the most empathetic presidents because he understood people's pain and wanted to do what he could to take it away, comforting people who were hurt and praising when they succeeded. He was fortunate enough to have his grandmother's guidance to help him understand the lie and move from resentment to compassion.

YOU ARE ON A HIGHER PLANE

We've seen the many ways in which resentment imprisons us in the past, fueling anger, revenge, and envy. It destroys peace of mind. It holds back love. It kills trust. And it fuels self-righteousness, blinding us to our own imperfections.

Of course, nobody could blame us for being resentful. We weren't given the advantages of a peaceful, loving home, and over the years the resentments we justifiably felt carried into the present—resentments that for many accumulate until they explode into retaliatory strikes against others or self-destructive behavior that swallows up the possibility of happiness. So many children of domestic violence become territorial and vengeful, without really understanding why.

So what can we do to erase the constant replay of old grudges? How can we release feelings of regret and blame, and heal the injustice of what we endured?

As people who've endured domestic violence as children, we have the perceptive abilities to see what's going on with others. So when resentment triggers, if we remember to step back from the situation, we can use those skills to see the bigger picture and cultivate a sense of curiosity about others. The more we do this, the less likely we are to feel resentment and the pathway to empathy and compassion is more clear.

This process can then lead us to forgive ourselves and allow us to dissolve resentment for good. Remember what Cloé Madanes told me: "People who experience an injustice in childhood, one brought on by their parents, feel a spiritual pain that shapes the unconscious. Because of what they experienced, they are able to reach a plane that few humans can, a level of understanding, resilience, and compassion that resides deep inside them."

Consider this story from Mother Teresa:

> I once picked up a woman from a garbage dump and she was burning with fever; she was in her last days and her only lament was: "My son did this to me." I begged her: "You must forgive your son. In a moment of madness, when he was not himself, he did a thing he regrets. Be a mother to him, forgive him." It took me a long time to make her say: "I forgive my son." Just before she died in my arms, she was able to say that with a real forgiveness. She was not concerned that she was dying. The breaking of the heart was that her son did not want her. This is something you and I can understand.[13]

The stories of Janine, Marina, even this dying woman from the slums of India, highlight the choice that lies at the heart of compassion. In the end, it's a decision that we must make for ourselves—to *cut the ties with the past* that allow others to continue hurting us long after the true harm is done. It takes strength to recognize our pain as something that belongs to us alone and to take ownership of it. It takes courage to recognize that hanging on to pain is just a way of punishing ourselves further. And most of all, it takes compassion to rise above our own pain and discover that the people who have hurt us are often deeply wounded themselves. That's precisely why Mahatma Gandhi believed that "the weak can never forgive. Forgiveness is an attribute of the strong."[14]

Janine has taken that lesson to heart, and allowed it to help her grow emotionally and spiritually. She has become a fabulously successful consultant and turned around the bitterness of her past: "I never thought I could forgive anyone for what happened to me—I didn't want to forgive. But once I took the first step, I felt so much better.

"It's taken me a long time to realize that most people are carrying around their own pain. When someone tries to hurt me these days, I have a completely different attitude. Before I might have tried to hurt them right back—that was my killer instinct. But now I realize that they have probably been hurt in some way too. That insight—learning that truth—makes me realize that I really wouldn't want to go back and try to change my life. My childhood happened for a reason and it has made me stronger than ever."

YOUR FIRST STEP: KNOW FOR CERTAIN AT YOUR CORE YOU ARE GOOD

We all have this compassion deep within us. Anyone who grew up living with domestic violence understands pain better than most and they have the capacity to respond with empathy and compassion toward another who is hurting. It is natural to us. It's a tool we can use for good. Even though throughout our lives, yours and mine, we have done things that we are not proud of. Things that make us question ourselves and ask, "Deep down am I a good person?" Yes, you are. I say that because I believe that I know how you would answer this question: Would you help a child who was lost in a park?

I took my son to the park to go fishing for the first time. Afterward, we went to get ice cream, and I saw just one table by the lake that was free. It would create the perfect moment. I noticed a person heading over to the table, so I sped over with my son to get the table. But now I had to go get the ice cream. My son was only four, so it was not a good idea to leave him there, but since I didn't want anyone else to have our table I told him to stay there, and that I would be right back. As I made the decision, I knew deep down that it was not right.

I went around the corner to get the ice cream, and when I came back, my son was gone. As any parent knows, it's terrifying. All kinds of possibilities run through your mind as you search frantically for your child. I finally spotted him. He had roamed rather far from the table. He was standing next to a man, holding his hand. After my initial relief, my mind flashed with all the negative emotions as I walked toward them: fear, anger, guilt, worthlessness, and resentment. I felt like a bad father, guilty and angry with myself, and had to offset that emotion by casting blame. Why? Because it was my fault for so long as a child, it could never be my fault as an adult. First, I blamed my son.

"Where were you? I told you to stay put. If you hadn't wandered off this never would have happened!"

As my son stood closer to the man, hugging his leg, my resentment turned toward the stranger. Who was this guy, stepping into my role as father and protector? Shooting him a menacing look,

I said, "This is my son. It's fine. I can take it from here." I didn't even thank the man.

But then he smiled at me kindly, completely unfazed by my hostile body language. "These things happen," he said nervously. "Please excuse me, but that is my bus," and then he sprinted off toward the bus stop that was about a football field away in the distance.

In that instant, I wondered who this man was who would risk missing his bus to help a lost little boy in the park. And by contrast, who was I to not even thank him? To blame him? Who was I? My curiosity about another person helped me step outside of myself and led me to a state of heightened awareness. Suddenly, all those negative emotions that culminated in resentment just melted away. I realized that immediate reaction came from a past of hurt, making me harsh with others because I was harshest on myself. I was resentful because I lacked compassion for myself.

But now I could see that this man was a good person. He did something selfless, out of kindness and concern for a little boy in distress. So, I had to ask myself, Would I have done the same?

I believed I would stop too. Most people would. I would help a child in a way that I was never helped and so would you.

Take a moment and feel what that man must have felt as his hand held the hand of a child in need, looking into those tear-stained eyes and feeling a wave of protective tenderness. That feeling is your goodness. That is who you are. Deep down we are worthwhile. No matter what happens, that essence of you as a human being that you would stop and do that, no matter what happens in life, no matter how worthless you believe yourself to be. It is hard to deny that you would help that child, *especially* after what you have been through in your own childhood. That is who you are. It is essential to remember this. You cannot have compassion for others unless you have it for yourself. You are worthwhile and someone should have taken away your pain. The next best thing is for you to take it away, which is exactly what you are doing as you read these words. You now have compassion for what you experienced. That means you can have compassion for others.

FROM THE LIE TO THE TRUTH

The Lie

You are not a good person deep down because you resent others and their happiness. You must live in resentment and bitterness toward those who hurt you, with buried rage eating at you. Your resentment will make them hurt, and you will feel better. You can't move forward; you can't release the past and are stuck in a pattern of reliving old anger, triggered by the envy of others.

The Why

Because of what you experienced as a child living with domestic violence, you are prone to resentment—the accumulation of anger that has gone unexpressed. In many cases, that anger couldn't be released in the moment, so you relive it. It then gets channeled toward others. Anyone who had a childhood has something you never had, which can lead to thoughts like, "It wasn't fair, they don't deserve it, I hope they fail." Resentment is a simmering fury that comes from the endless replay of that old anger over and over again.

The Truth

I am compassionate.

I now know that someone should have taken away my pain, but I also know that only those who have truly suffered can understand what suffering feels like. Because of this I have reached a plane that few humans can reach.

I do not cause pain in others. I naturally want to help take the pain away. This is the essence of compassion.

And since I know that the feeling of resentment causes unneeded pain inside of me, since I know that I am a good person inside, I do not create this pain inside myself by indulging in a feeling of resentment.

I am compassionate, and today if a feeling of resentment comes over me, I immediatly remind myself of these truths.

To Try

1. If you identify a feeling of resentment coming over you do two things:

   - Remind yourself that you are at your core a good person and recall the feeling that you felt when you imagined yourself helping a child in need. (Or think of the story about my son in the park.)
   - Remind yourself that you have reached a plane that most humans can't; those who have suffered understand suffering.

2. You have an ability to understand what people are feeling and you can activate that gift by cultivating your curiosity and asking a question like, Why do you ask?

This allows you to get to someone's true intent. Use this curiosity to find something to praise or openly admire about the other person.

3. Choose to forgive for your own sake. You can start the process of forgiving others—and yourself—by simply imagining yourself saying the words. You can begin by asking your parents, What was your childhood like? Remember this question is not as much for them as it is for you.

4

SAD TO GRATEFUL

They prefer the certainty of misery rather than the
misery of uncertainty.   —Bruce Perry, MD, PhD

When Savannah's mother, Rowena, married a military man, she thought her family's future was secure. A glamorous woman with a professional singing career, Rowena always sought out men in uniform for their military benefits: better housing, health care, and good schools for Savannah and her younger brothers, yet Savannah wasn't even sure if she even liked these men.

When Savannah's second stepfather came into her life when she was thirteen, he imposed a kind of martial law enforced with violence, and Savannah and her siblings were sometimes the targets. Even the most trivial incidents would send him over the edge. The family had ordered pizza from Domino's, and her little half brother, who was three at the time, reached up to the counter to grab a cinnamon stick without asking first. When the toddler accidentally knocked them all to the floor, Savannah's stepfather picked him up by his arm and held him up in the air. Their mother screamed at him to stop, and he lunged for her instead. Savannah ran into the bathroom, grabbed a hair dryer and used it to hit her stepfather in the head, hoping it would stun him enough to release his grip on her mother. More enraged, he tossed her brother onto the ground to grab Savannah by the throat and slammed her against the wall.

She still remembers him trying to strangle both her and her mother with each hand. Then suddenly he stopped. He dropped both women and walked out without a word.

"There were no apologies; everything went back to normal the next day, and that's how it always was. Nothing ever seemed to get better."

Savannah's turbulent childhood of living with domestic violence was the only consistent thing in her family's uncertain existence as they moved in and out of military bases all over the United States and Europe. It left her with a deep sadness and sense of loss that she's still dealing with today. While most of the violence took place between her mother and stepfather, life revolved around his strict rules to the point at which she became the live-in nanny, servant, and cook. Still just a child herself, she was cast in the role of mother to her younger siblings, isolated in her own home and robbed of her freedom, her childhood. Subject to constant criticism and discipline, she felt completely insignificant, even to her own mother. She was told she was good for nothing and had to earn the roof over her head by doing her parents' bidding, and she came to believe that her life would always be this way.

"I had way too much information about how dark life could get," she says, "and not enough ground to stand on. I couldn't carry it all."

I LOST SOMETHING I CANNOT GET BACK—
MY CHILDHOOD

For many children of domestic violence, feeling sad is a constant that follows them well into adulthood. You might call the deep feeling of sadness, loss, depression, or misery. You feel defeated, let down, or grief stricken. Perhaps you go through life turned inward, dwelling on the hopelessness of your situation and thinking, "What's the point? Nothing good is ever going to happen to me anyway." While this feeling may vary by degrees from being blue to suffering clinical depression, for the sake of simplicity we'll call it sadness.

As a child I felt let down often. Things just didn't work out for me. My mother let me down, my family let me down, everyone let me down because they didn't help me or protect me. I lost my childhood. I had a deep sense of loss around that and it made me sad.

Like an umbrella under which many other emotions fall, feeling sad is a common feeling for anyone who grew up living with domestic violence. Crippling and complex, it is an insidious affliction that immobilizes its victims, making them feel persistently depressed, unhappy, and hopeless. Different from just the normal blues, depression is an all-encompassing low mood that destroys the pleasure you would ordinarily take in enjoyable activities. Hanging over your world is the constant sense of dread.

Children can be trapped in sadness, unable to understand or articulate it. It's the quicksand of emotions, making you sink deeper and deeper into a world of despair. Research increasingly links the risk of depression to the number of uncontrollable stressful events people experienced during their childhood.[1] So you withdraw and become isolated. As a child, you hide in your room. You lose yourself in watching TV or playing video games. And if you're an adult, you may numb yourself with sleeping pills, alcohol, or other drugs. You're often angry, lashing out at those you perceive as weaker than you. And you don't consistently function well in school, in extracurricular activities, or at social events.

VIOLENCE KNOWS NO GENDER

Even before Savannah's violent stepfather came along, she had no foundation for happiness. Anger, despair, and abandonment—that was what she'd always known.

Rowena, her mother, also had a violent side. Her first husband, Savannah's birth father, ran off when Savannah was a baby because his wife was physically abusive toward him. Rowena's second husband, a sweet-natured guy Savannah came to think of as Dad, was more loving and never abusive, but he was an alcoholic who spent most of his time in bars near the military base when he wasn't working night shifts. Savannah's mother was also a heavy drinker who liked to party, often leaving Savannah and her younger half brother with neighbors and relatives. Her mother was so neglectful that a neighbor once reported the situation to social services, and Savannah and her younger brother almost got taken into foster care.

It got so bad on the military base in Europe where they were living at the time that her parents became known as "the Drop-Offs" because they were always trying to drop their children off somewhere so they could go out for the night. "It was so embarrassing," recalls Savannah. Not only was it obvious to her that her parents either didn't care enough to be responsible or were incapable of looking after their own children, everyone in the small community of the base knew.

Savannah's mother rarely expressed affection toward her children. In fact, her nurturing skills were practically nonexistent. She wasn't physically abusive, at least not with Savannah and her brother, but she communicated almost exclusively through sarcastic remarks and put-downs.

"This was not anything intentional; to be mean or degrading, but this is how my mother behaved. This is how she spoke," recalls Savannah. "This is how she taught me to speak."

When Savannah was twelve, the family moved back to the United States. By then, her mother's second marriage was finished, although they tried to make it work for a few months after her stepfather's affair. Because their mother stayed behind in Europe, Savannah and her brother moved to a military base with her stepfather in Oregon. They settled into their new life in America, and for a moment it looked as if there were hope.

Even though her parents were now estranged, Savannah remained close with her first stepfather, and came to know his extended family as her own. She and her brother stayed with him while her mother took off again. Life without her was noticeably better. But the peace and stability ended when her mother finally came back with a newborn baby by the next military man, her new husband-to-be.

"I could not fathom why she would decide that of all the things we needed right now, some random man she met was supposed to be the answer to our problems," recalls Savannah, who questioned her mother's decision.

"Aren't you going through something since you just had a baby? Like, postpartum or whatever? I don't think you should be making decisions like this so soon, Mom."

"And what am I supposed to do now with the baby and no husband? Your stepfather and I are getting divorced. We can't live here anymore. Base housing will kick us out, and we will be homeless. But I gotta plan."

She left a few weeks later for Indiana, where her new boyfriend was stationed. Savannah didn't see her new brother again until he was three months old, when her mother sent for Savannah and her other brother.

Savannah had a bad feeling. She was aware that being around her mother, getting dragged along as she made questionable life choices, was becoming toxic. So she begged her stepfather to adopt her. He gave her a hug, told her he was sorry and that he didn't want to lose her but explained that the law wouldn't allow him to. It felt like another rejection. Instead of seeing the facts, she concluded that he was just making up a story because he didn't care.

As we grow older, it becomes very easy for us to become disappointed in others. If someone doesn't deliver on a promise, it becomes a personal affront. We figure, "This is what happens to people like me." It's hard enough to deal with the world letting you down, but it adds an entire new level of challenge and difficulty when you believe that everyone who lets you down is doing it with malice directed at you. It's one more thing that reinforces the lie of our relentless sadness.

Life got progressively worse for Savannah and her brothers. Despite the escalating violence, her mother always took her new stepfather's side. Savannah felt torn between defending her mother, who sought her protection, and total rejection, when her mother and new stepfather blamed her for getting in the way. Savannah felt there was no way out, and she fell into a deep depression.

IS THE SADNESS SO BAD THAT PHYSICALLY HURTING YOURSELF FEELS BETTER?

When Savannah was fourteen, the cutting started. She began the almost daily ritual of slicing a razor blade across her arms until the blood flowed as she tried to release the chronic emotional hurt.

It's difficult to say how many people who've lived with domestic violence have harmed themselves, because it usually takes place in secret, but it is more common than you would think. According to a UK study published in 2006, about 25 percent of emergency room patients with a history of domestic violence presented evidence of self-harm.[2] Many of the people we come into contact with at our foundation report starting rituals of cutting themselves in their early teens.

The psychological pain of growing up in these homes is so deep, that physical pain can induce a sense of temporary relief, much the same as abusing drugs or alcohol. In fact, many of these practices go hand in hand when we are so deep in this sadness we see no way out. It's what can happen when we find ourselves deep inside the lie of sadness and despair.

Self-injury—the act of deliberately harming your own body, involves systematically cutting, burning, or otherwise injuring yourself as a way to manage tension, anger, frustration, a sense of chaos, or any emotion that's difficult to control.[3] It can even help temporarily break through that sense of numbness that accompanies some forms of severe depression. Savannah describes the relief of the ritual best:

> It was more than a coping mechanism; it was a way of
> life for me—clothing choices in the summer; music

> styles in my headphones; writing from my heart; blood
> on the pages. It gave me a release every time someone
> hurt me. It was a way of keeping my anger in control.
> Instead of hurting others, I would hurt myself.

It was the one area of her life that was hers alone. She'd go into the privacy of her room, lock the door and play her favorite music, especially selected for the ritual of cutting up and down her arms with a blade. She even kept a secret box with her cutting equipment and a diary where she wrote about all the experiences and emotional pain she was trying to relieve.

But at school and among her friends, she put up a brave front, flirting with boys, partying, and drinking whenever she had the opportunity. No one knew how much she was hurting.

"I would pretend to be bold and sassy in public, getting the lead in every play. I was on the dance team in high school. I became the director of our school's TV news station. I even tried to run for class president my senior year. But when I got back home, I felt that I was just an insignificant part of my family."

TRYING TO NUMB THE PAIN LEADS NOWHERE

When they moved overseas, Savannah was completely trapped. Her new stepfather was high ranking and had a lot of power on the base, and he kept tight control over his family. Whenever Savannah made new friends, all her movements were monitored. Apart from school, she had to remain at home to take care of the kids and do chores. She loved the theater, and got involved in the school play, but by the time any production got to the performance stage, her stepfather ordered her to stay home. She met her first serious boyfriend, who spoke his mind to Savannah's mother about the situation at home, and was banned from ever seeing him again.

Savannah added shoplifting to her list of escapist habits, and the drinking and drug taking escalated. She tried more positive ways to manage the sadness, and even began going to church, but when she was caught stealing, her stepfather banned her from Sunday services as well.

"He told me, 'You're just a fuckup, nothing can fix you, not even God,' and I let that be my mentality."

At nineteen, Savannah made her escape, working at a factory off the base to save up just enough cash for a plane ticket. That job was her only freedom, because her stepfather kept close tabs on her shifts and monitored her so carefully that if she didn't make it home by a certain time, Savannah would catch hell.

Once out of Germany, she landed at her grandmother's house in the Northeast, but they didn't get along, and by then her drug abuse was out of control. She spent the next year drifting back and forth across the country, eventually returning to her grandmother's house.

Friends and relatives tried to help, but with no home, no job, and not enough money or access to financial aid to go to college, she hit rock bottom. Savannah locked herself in her grandmother's spare bedroom and wrote *whore* in lipstick on the mirror. Blaring music, she drank "half a gallon" of vodka, smashed up the room, and started cutting herself. This time, she planned to go all the way and end her life.

As she was cutting, she looked over at a photo of herself cuddling in bed with her two younger brothers—the children she'd spent so much time caring for they called her Mom. In that moment, she couldn't do it. She loved them too much. They were the two people in the world she loved more than anyone, and that picture reminded her that they loved her back unconditionally; it was something to be grateful for. Smeared in her own blood, she dropped the knife and called to her grandmother for help.

SERVING ANOTHER TOOK HER OUT OF SADNESS

Savannah was still a long way from healing, but that brief glimpse at the truth that she had something to be grateful for saved her life. With so much overwhelming sadness and loss dominating her life, she still had it within her to see that there was something for her to be grateful for. She was able to ask and answer for herself, "What is great about this?" Yes, "what is wrong" you can always clearly see, but "what is great" is also just as easily available, if you ask. On the beach in Oregon watching the moon, at school in Germany, working with her theater friends, and briefly enjoying the fellowship of the church on the military base, Savannah was able to feel gratitude in the simplest things. She, more than anyone, appreciated those brief moments of light because they were so rare in the dark world she grew up in. Most of all she was grateful to finally be out of that house.

Numerous studies have shown that gratitude for the more positive aspects of our lives is the key to arriving at a new truth. It's not so much a feeling as an attitude that we can consciously cultivate and that brings real and measurable benefits to our mental health.[4] Adopting a grateful attitude becomes a method for rediscovering all the things we can easily overlook in our lives—the kindness of others and the hidden beauty in the very smallest things. As we look beyond ourselves and see the world through a new lens, life changes for the better. Savannah had glimpses of it, it was just a matter of learning how to sustain the attitude long enough to turn it into her truth.

For almost two years after her aborted suicide attempt, Savannah drifted and experienced more setbacks. She was seeking happiness in all the wrong places—with men who were violent, emotionally abusive, drug dealers, or all of the above. They were all different versions of the stepfather she ran away from. Finally, at twenty-one, Savannah found herself in Seattle—pregnant, malnourished, and determined to get away from the father of the child. "There was no way was I going to bring a child into another abusive relationship," she says.

She remembered she had an uncle living ten minutes from where she was staying. As soon as he heard her voice on the phone, he insisted she come to his house and stay for as long as it took to get well.

Savannah terminated her pregnancy and spent the next three weeks in his spare bedroom, sleeping, crying, and succumbing to her despair. The grief for her lost childhood and the opportunities she'd missed was overwhelming. Finally, her uncle had had enough. He dragged her out of bed, stood her in front of the mirror and said, "Look at yourself! You are beautiful. You have so much promise in life and all the wisdom to become successful and happy. You have a whole amazing life ahead of you. I need you to see that."

Savannah's uncle became the One for her, reminding her of all the many things she had to be grateful for: the fact that she was intelligent and worldly, with more life experience and sophistication attained in her twenty-one years than most people have in their lifetime; that she was young and healthy; and that there were people in her life who cared about her.

One afternoon, her uncle brought home a bunch of helium

balloons. They went into the backyard of their brownstone, and he made her write everything she hated about herself, all her problems, on the balloons. One by one, she let them float up into the air. When she'd released them all, she felt physically lighter.

She cleaned herself up, got her hair done, went shopping for new clothes and then hit the pavement. Savannah is so attractive, she even did some modeling. But she quickly found work as a hostess at a fine restaurant, eventually working her way up to manager of an elite nightclub. And she stopped cutting herself.

From that moment in her uncle's backyard, when she let go of all that pain and sadness, Savannah's transformation was remarkably rapid. Today, just three years later, Savannah is happily married and living a full life with a career she loves. She keeps her friends close, exchanging positive and encouraging texts and email messages every day. She's also grateful—*for everything*.

"I don't want to change anything about what happened to me. I am not mad about it anymore. I believe in my heart that everything happens for a reason."

These days, Savannah is the rock in her family. Her brothers, mother, extended family, and friends come to her for advice. She is the One for everyone her life touches.

"Had I not lived the life I lived I wouldn't know what to say or do in certain situations; I wouldn't know right from wrong. I wouldn't be so proud of myself had it all been handed to me."

Savannah expresses her gratitude by contributing. She shares her stories with others and uses her hard-won wisdom to help anyone who comes into her life. She's there for acquaintances, strangers, friends, even her mother, to listen and offer insight through her own experiences. She's learning to rein in her quick temper and manage the "tact and tone" problem she picked up from her mother, who loved to win an argument at all costs. In fact, she is conscious every moment of every day to be nothing like her mother or stepfather.

HURTING OTHERS CREATES THE ULTIMATE SADNESS

The first rule of dealing with sadness: Don't hurt the feelings or body of another when you get angry. Don't hurt them the way you were hurt. How many times have you felt justified in your mind to hurt someone's feelings only to find that a few minutes later you feel awful? If you hurt their body, it is even worse. That's because we are not designed to hurt those we love. When we do, we experience an equal hurt in the form of sadness and depression. But if you refrain from hurting others you won't have to feel this sadness. Of course, it's difficult to give when you feel you don't have much to give, just as it's difficult to give when no one was there for you. When you've grown up focused on all that you lost, you start to believe the lie: Life is bleak and it always will be. It's what you deserve. Then you try to escape the pain by going down a self-destructive path that serves only to reinforce the lie that there is nothing to be grateful for, and you are getting what you deserve.

There's a bleakness that becomes a part of our psychological and physiological makeup. People who've lived with domestic violence become conditioned for sadness through their unrelenting exposure to emotional stress, conflict, and neglect. Jack P. Shonkoff, director of the Center on the Developing Child, Harvard University, who has studied the biochemistry of stress and its impact on mood, explains that the human body contains a set of brain circuits and hormonal systems that are designed to deal with stress and threats to survival. But when we overtax these systems through constant exposure to domestic violence, they start to turn against us, constantly flooding our bodies with the stress hormones adrenaline and cortisone to create a broad range of behavioral and physiological disorders that can persist over a lifetime.

Many of the classic signs of depression—sleep disturbances, cognitive dullness, and a distinct loss of pleasure in everyday activities—will appear in children and adults even long after the storm of violence has passed.

WHEN YOU FOCUS ON YOURSELF, YOU WILL BE MISERABLE

Fiona struggled with sadness and depression her entire life after watching violence between her parents regularly as a child. Fiona grew up in an upscale neighborhood in New York State. Everyone knew her as an outgoing, vivacious girl who loved playing softball and field hockey but who was studious enough to make honor roll throughout middle school. School and sports were a passion for Fiona, and she was rewarded with praise and attention from friends, coaches, and teachers. No one noticed anything particularly wrong with Fiona—testimony at once to both her shame and courage.

Fiona's dad was the deacon of the local church and was admired by the community for his model family and principled sermons. That is, until Fiona and her mother turned up at the homeless shelter across town. A police restraining order was filed a week after they left their home. All the wealth and privilege of their past life couldn't help them. And without financial resources, Fiona and her mother had nowhere else to go.

Loyal parishioners urged the family to reconcile, but Fiona's mother refused. Fifteen grueling years—the secrets and the lies—had set her mind. More details emerged, dividing the church and making the local press. Fiona and her mother, with the help of family, eventually relocated in New Hampshire and began rebuilding their lives.

But Fiona's troubles followed her. She had kept herself together for years, just like her mother, maintaining the appearance of a happy family and finding an outlet in sports to redress her unhappiness. But after three weeks in the shelter, the embarrassment of what was said at school, and the move to a new town, Fiona began to crumble. She stopped eating, daydreamed through school, and quit calling her old friends. She skipped field hockey practices, complaining about her stomach, and hid in her room. She slept long hours, was listless throughout the weekends, and seemed uninterested in anything.

It was a dramatic change; under the strict discipline of her father, Fiona had always done well in school and been a good girl. But without his structure and all their family activities related to the church, Fiona felt lost and cut off from all she knew. She and her mother had escaped the abuse, but Fiona had been scarred much worse than anyone realized.

University of Michigan professor of psychology Sandra Graham-Bermann points out the marked disparity between child and adult behavior once they leave a violent environment. "While the adult often feels better right away, the child, who had to keep it together when the violence was happening, often falls apart,"

Graham-Bermann explained to us in an interview. "She feels sad and depressed because it's finally safe to do so—often for years to come."

Psychologists have long understood that all of our thinking, and even our most rudimentary observations, are emotionally charged. We see and understand the world through the lens of our own emotions. Depression often acts as a cognitive filter, distorting our perception of reality, a phenomenon that has been called *confirmation bias.* It simply means that sad people see sadness everywhere, because the depressed mind pays closer attention to whatever confirms a negative outlook and overlooks things that contradict it.

For Fiona, the glass was always half empty. She had a slow recovery, and several dramatic relapses during her early teens—weeks when she could barely manage to come out of her room. As she got older she became defiant—staying out late, becoming verbally abusive toward her mother, and sometimes binge drinking.

To break through the lie that says we must be sad, it's necessary to radically reshape our point of view. Those of us who grow up with domestic violence tend to be focused on ourselves because for so long we had to be; no one else was going to provide for our needs. At times we had to provide our own sense of security, love, and importance.

However, as long as you focus on yourself you will never be happy because you are not meeting your need for self-esteem. You don't feel good about yourself when you are serving only yourself. You feel best when you are doing something to help another person and are growing in the process. Because of what you have come through, you can help a child, your own children, or another adult who does not know what you know. You are an example. Discover that the purpose of your life is to be a powerful loving example of what is possible.

Fiona stumbled onto this truth almost by accident. She found an activity that awakened her sense of gratitude, showed her the truth about her own value to others, and helped pull her out of her depression. Volunteering with an older friend at an after-school special education center near her school, she earned externship credits toward a junior college degree in social work, but more important, she learned to feel grateful for what she had instead of mourning what she had lost.

"When I started working with autistic children, something about that whole experience just touched me. The look in their eyes when you show up, being someone else's window to the world, made me start to count *my own* blessings."

She began to see her own story in a more positive light—as someone whose survival made her stronger and gave her more to offer the world. She had suffered in childhood, but if these kids, who were facing even greater difficulties, could smile, then she could too. She could actually make their lives easier by helping them. The kids liked to see her every morning, and were sad when she missed a day. Just knowing that she had touched someone's life made her feel grateful for what she had and what she could still offer the world.

As her outlook brightened, she started connecting more with her mother. They both still have a lot of deep hurt and anger to sort out together, but her mother noticed a clear change in Fiona's attitude. By the time Fiona entered her senior year in high school, she had actually broken out her old softball glove—a gift from her dad—and began playing on the school's intramural team again. Her grades improved as well.

Fiona realized that she couldn't stop her thoughts from happening; she'll never be totally immune to a sad thought. But now she knows that she's got a choice. She can exercise a sense of control that she never knew as a child, when her father's unpredictable outbursts and violence left her in constant fear. Now she can choose how long she stays in the sadness.

She didn't have that power to control her reactions when she was a child, because her underdeveloped neocortex wouldn't allow her to reason maturely. Unlike adults, who will use logic and reason to process the meaning of an event, young children understand only its emotional content. They can't put any distance between what they see and how they feel. They are simply overwhelmed with pain and sadness at seeing their loved ones getting hurt over and over again. But now, as an adult, Fiona can change that perspective by combating sad thoughts with grateful ones. She has turned the practice of gratitude into a conscious, everyday effort, by making it a habit to consider exactly what she's most grateful for *today*. By starting her day acknowledging the things for which she is most grateful, she sends her mind down new avenues of thought, seeking out the positive aspects she can look forward to. She opens up new neural pathways for thinking and diverts her mind from the false conclusions that were imprinted upon her as a child.

It's made a massive difference in her life. These days, Fiona is married with two kids. Fiona's happy, and it shows in her face.

"When things get bad," she says, "you have to take a step back. You have to keep things relative. I've got my kids, my husband, and my friends. That's what matters. And I always know that nothing we're going to face tomorrow holds a candle to what I had to live through back then . . . nothing."

Fiona's truth echoes what the latest research has revealed: We have the capacity to experience joy precisely because of what we have lived through. As psychology professor Sonja Lyubomirsky, puts it: "People who have experienced adversity, for example several negative events or life changing moments, are ultimately happier and less distressed, traumatized, stressed or impaired than those who have experienced no adversity."[5]

Fiona and Savannah are both living proof that you don't have to believe the lie of profound sadness. In their own way, each was affected by sadness and loss, but each made a choice, refusing to accept the lie created in childhood. They took action by recognizing that the past did not have to be their whole story. Even through all the bad things, they had the potential within them to recognize and appreciate the good—a gratitude for the smallest gifts was their secret weapon. They even see their childhood as something to be grateful for because it has given them the inner strength and wisdom to serve others: Fiona through her work with autistic children; Savannah as a sister, friend, wife, and daughter who can offer understanding and compassion because of all that she has lived through.

FROM THE LIE TO THE TRUTH

The Lie

Feeling sad is a constant that will always be with you. Things can be going great, but then a few minutes later, you sink into a sadness and cannot get out. This is just how you are. You go through life *focused on yourself*. You consciously and subconsciously mourn the loss of your childhood.

The Why

As a child of domestic violence you feel as though you lost something: love from your parents, your childhood, important relationships, and so on. You believe you are destined in life to continue to experience loss and hurt. This sadness is made worse when you hurt others. When you hurt someone with words or otherwise, especially those you love, you cannot feel good about yourself.

After leaving a violent environment, adults often feel better right away. The children, on the other hand, who had to keep it together when the violence was happening, often feel the effects for the rest of their lives. They may now act out on their feelings because they sense it is finally safe to do so—and the sadness they feel may continue for years to come.

The Truth

I am grateful. Today, I will take the time to feel those things for which I am most grateful.

I remind myself that I now know the truth. I am no longer in the environment of my childhood. I can sleep through the night. I am now in control of my life. The very things that I longed for years ago are now available to me in abundance. They are mine. For that I am grateful.

I serve others. Gratitude comes to life through service without expectation of anything in return. I guard against hurting the feelings of others because it always makes me sad in return.

I begin my day and ask myself throughout, What am I grateful for? What is great about this?

To Try

1. When you feel the urge to do or say something hurtful toward another, break the pattern that your brain is in by saying aloud to yourself, "I am above this. This is not me. It's just a pattern." You were born to take pain away and not to be the cause of it.

2. When you find yourself feeling sad and notice that you are too focused on yourself, take an action that serves another. Call someone and tell her you were thinking about her. Ask someone how his day is going and really take the time to listen. Anything that makes another person feel important and appreciated.

3. Contribute beyond yourself. I know it's difficult to give when you feel you don't have much to give; that is why it is so powerful. It doesn't need to take much time. You can become a role model for another because of what you have come through; you can help another child of domestic violence, your own child, or another adult who does not know what you know. Create a schedule that allows you to consistently serve another: once a day, once a week, or even just an hour a month. The key is to schedule simple actions that create the habit.

4. Use DATA, a tool I will introduce in Chapter 6, to control anger, and you will not experience the sadness that is the inevitable by-product.

5

ALONE TO TRUSTING

Their brain was trained from an early age to assume negative intent. They learn not to trust.

—David Sousa, *How the Brain Learns*

To look at Eleanor, no one would guess how alone she felt. Beautiful and popular, she's surrounded by friends; she has a loving boyfriend and even maintains a positive relationship with the parents who raised her, despite having grown up living with domestic violence. She is bright, successful, and accomplished, and yet for most of her life, she's struggled to let people in.

"It's not anyone else's job to worry about me or take care of me, and I know that I can be a lot to deal with. So I try to work through my issues within myself."

The lie of being alone for some is about not being in an intimate relationship and for some is more about feeling unconnected to others. You don't have as many good friends as you would like, or those in your circle don't feel like true friends. Somehow, you always feel separate from the rest of the world. You don't trust in yourself; you don't know yourself; so how can you trust others?.

That's how I felt throughout most of my life. I had dated only two girls until the time I was eighteen, and I wasn't intimate with either of them. It wasn't that I didn't want them; I just couldn't fathom for the life of me why they would want to be intimate with me. Then, at nineteen, I met my future wife. Things got physical, and I fell madly in love. One night I opened up to her and shared some of the details of my childhood. I knew this was risky. I told her how afraid I was of so many things. How we only have so much time to live. How the idea of dying petrifies me. But she was not comfortable talking about it. So I decided not to speak of it again. Not until twenty years later did we briefly discuss it, and that was with our marriage counselor when we were two weeks away from getting divorced.

How could we not have talked about it? Is it that shameful? How could I not share? How could she not ask? I know if we had talked about it years ago, we would be together today. Not being able to trust enough to share—not knowing then what I know now—is my greatest regret. One of my greatest wishes for you is that you avoid making the same mistake.

———

Maybe you don't feel capable of maintaining a relationship and are uncertain that other people want to be with you. You may even avoid intimacy. There's a sense of disconnect from others or a suspicion of their motives. Perhaps you simply feel that you are on your own. You had no one to rely on but yourself growing up, and you assume that will always be the case. Either way, you lack trust in yourself and, because of that, find it next to impossible to trust in others.

Eleanor was always an independent spirit. Shortly after she was born, in the Northwest, Eleanor's mother moved herself and her daughter back to the Midwest to be near family. She'd completely broken off her relationship with Eleanor's birth father, a military man, to raise her child on her own. But she soon met Johnnie, the man who would become Eleanor's stepfather, and the only father figure she'd ever known.

Eleanor's earliest memories of violence occurred when she was three. "It was the middle of the night, and I woke up to this huge commotion in the living room," she recalls. "I ran in to see what was going on and saw my stepdad viciously beating my mother. Mom yelled at me to get help and for a moment I froze, until my stepdad turned to face me."

Eleanor, still little more than a toddler, ran to her grandparents' house a few doors down. She was too embarrassed to explain to them what happened, sensing it was something shameful, but somehow they coaxed it out of her and called 911. The police came and escorted her stepfather away from the house. But of course Johnnie returned and the abuse continued on and off until Eleanor turned seventeen.

Johnnie never put his hands on Eleanor. As is the case for the majority of those who grow up living with domestic violence, she was not the target. Typically, he would get drunk and the fighting would begin, usually in the middle of the night. Eleanor would wake up and try to get her stepfather off her mother, and he would respond by shoving her out of the way and screaming verbal abuse.

"He'd say things to me like, 'You're just a fucking nuisance; you'll never be worth shit.' He made it clear I was in his way."

Her stepfather didn't have to be drunk to turn violent; the anger could erupt anytime. She begged her mother to leave him, and she tried a few times, but she could never let go. "They had this weird codependent thing going on. My mother thought he needed her." Eleanor tried to explain to her mother that she needed her too.

When it got really bad, Eleanor would go to her boyfriend's house. They knew what was going on but no questions were asked. It wasn't that they weren't concerned so much as they knew not to go there. "I was just so embarrassed," recalls Eleanor. "Like there was something wrong with me."

As she got older and stronger and her stepfather became increasingly frail from alcoholism and self-neglect, Eleanor could better protect her mother and wrestle him away from her.

Eleanor was in control; she had to be. Her relationships became subject to stringent standards. Friends had to prove themselves and meet the high bar she set because, as she says, "I would not accept anything less." She poured herself into her studies and athletic activities. She was captain on every debate and academic team as well as every sports club. Her involvement in extracurricular activities was her escape. She was also determined to do everything she needed to do to have a comfortable life where she could provide for her family and be the opposite of her stepfather.

"I hated him more than anything and anybody when I was growing up. I wanted to be his polar opposite," says Eleanor. "Even when I was little I declared I would never let my family go through that. I think that's why I strive so hard to be successful."

I FEEL ALONE

Eleanor graduated from college and now works as a project engineer in the Southeast, where she also plans to pursue an MBA. She is in a relationship with an understanding and compassionate young man, who is making it much easier for her to be trusting.

It's not that her adult life has been tragic or dysfunctional. Far from it—she got out and turned herself around in remarkable ways. But as long as she can remember, Eleanor has felt a weight, as if all the joy in her life has been muffled. She is only just beginning to take a step back and see how her childhood has affected her, and in doing so she realizes how many others have experienced what she did.

In relationships, she's always been giving. When people pass the test and meet her standards—when she's certain they're nothing like her stepfather—she loves hard. But until now she hasn't necessarily allowed herself to trust in love received. Eleanor has even struggled to trust herself. Although her instincts are sharp, she continually questions them, lacking that inner certainty when it comes to relationships that, until recently, were volatile. Eleanor was always too quick to react to a perceived transgression, quick to assume the worst about the intentions of others.

"I always knew the right answer but would second-guess myself anyway," she says. "I am only just now getting to the point where I can follow my first thought without hesitation."

Her newfound clarity has helped her see the connection between this lack of certainty and the pain of witnessing her mother—a woman she admires and respects—continually putting herself in a situation in which she was hurt. In every other respect, her mother was the backbone and primary support of the household, an educated and intelligent woman who trained in a medical field and sometimes works as many as three jobs. Eleanor's mother always told her that this did not have to be her life, and she is constantly apologizing for everything she put her daughter through. But her mother's self-destructive choices led Eleanor to question everything.

Now, the growing trust she has in herself, and her newfound

ability to share, is inspiring her to become the One for others. She's begun with her own family. Although they are far from friends, Eleanor feels "oddly protective" over her stepfather in his weakened condition. She's since come to learn that he too was a child of domestic violence.

"My mom comes first, but if my stepfather needs me I am there for him too, which is weird," she says, second-guessing herself again.

Even last spring, when she went to visit her birth father for the first time, Eleanor felt protective of the family who raised her. It was a happy reunion, and she was glad to meet her half-siblings and see where she came from. As a child she used to look at his photograph and pray that he would come and save her, but she didn't share the story of her past with him because she didn't want him to know how badly her mother was doing.

"She was on her own; she did what she could," she says.

Eleanor has always been the hero and protector in her family. As hard as she has found it to let others in, she is overflowing with compassion for others. She volunteers through her sorority to mentor young girls and help them with their self-esteem. She's a coach for junior high track and field. At college, she participated in a public service program that identified troubled sixth graders and brought them to campus for mentoring and friendship. It's work that Eleanor plans to continue.

"I want to be that person I wanted to have in my life and let them know that everything they need they have inside of them," says Eleanor.

She was that person. Like many who grew up living with domestic violence, Eleanor has always seemed remarkably well adjusted. No one would guess what she's lived through. And yet she always felt alone, never able to open up or give herself completely, struggling to believe that someone could love and accept her for who she was. She gave, but she could never receive. She was the strong one for others, but never allowed herself to lean on anyone else and kept even those she loved at arm's length. No one could reach her all the way. But then she found her rock— someone she could truly trust. Her boyfriend and his mother became the Ones for Eleanor. As the family she'd always wanted, they made her feel safe enough to open up and share all that she'd been through. For the first time in her life, she felt a deep connection to another.

"It feels as if a fire had been rekindled, like I have more oxygen. My light is shining just a little bit brighter now that I've learned I don't have to carry all that baggage around."

As someone who lived with domestic violence, the seeds of trust, the desire to let others in, were what ultimately drove her. Buried underneath the lie is always the truth. Her recognition that she could allow herself to be vulnerable because she was vulnerable as a child for so long and successfully came through it—came through it stronger—became her secret weapon. It taught her just how important it was to be trustworthy and trusting. She now sees how allowing herself to be vulnerable is a key to trust.

KEEPING OTHERS AT A DISTANCE FEELS SAFER

Eleanor is a highly successful individual, a model of strength and courage who never saw herself as a victim, but even she was holding herself back from truly connecting with others. Some of the lies still plague her. She'd spent so many years striving to be the opposite of what she experienced growing up, putting all her energy into loving and protecting those she cared about most, and yet she suffered from one of the most pervasive lies among children of domestic violence: that they are and will be fundamentally alone.

All of the lies that we've already explored are often closely intertwined with a profound sense of social isolation. Sometimes, it's self-inflicted. These children and adults just don't feel safe with others, and understandably so. When the person on whom their entire lives depend is under attack or behaves unpredictably and sometimes cruelly, their own emotional world is thrown into turmoil, and it's hard to feel safe with anyone.

Children of domestic violence grow up believing the lie that it's safer to be alone. Studies clearly show that they have fewer relationships than others and far more difficulty as adults in achieving intimacy.[1] They find it difficult to make strong emotional connections. They learn that life is easier and better when they keep people at a distance and their feelings locked away. As childhood trauma expert Bruce Perry says, "The most traumatic aspects of all disasters involves the shattering of human connections."[2]

Brain expert David Sousa reports that many children rescued from extremely violent homes and placed into foster homes immediately retreat into a shell. They don't have the ability to appreciate other people's good intentions because their experience taught them to see everyone as a potential threat. Their mirror neuron system was never given the chance to develop, so they see every adult as an enemy, as a potential antagonist.

"Might this set them up to assume a negative intent?" Sousa

asks. "Will every stimuli received from this person be viewed through this lens? It's how their brains perceived an environment it was never designed for in the first place," he told me.

The irony is that when these individuals do place their trust in others, they can actually find great happiness and fulfillment in their lives.

It took me a long time to arrive at this truth. Growing up, I had friends, of course, although I never thought of them as especially close. They'd come over to whatever rental house we were in at the moment, but I was never comfortable with it. At one level, I was just too ashamed of how different our house was to them. We were poor, our house was a wreck, and I never knew if Keith might be around.

Instead, my friendships were conducted often near their homes. If I was lucky, sometimes I might get myself invited over to someone's house for dinner, where I always tried to leave a good impression, so I could get invited back again. But truth be told, I never really had *close* friends as a kid.

I admired the kids who were lucky enough to say they had a best friend because I could never imagine anyone liking me that much. I never dared call someone else my best friend for fear that he would make fun of me for saying so. I simply had trouble trusting, and out of fear of being rejected, I pushed people away and spent a lot of time alone.

At the time, I rationalized my isolation. If I didn't have many friends, I told myself it was because I was the loner type. If I had to fend for myself at home because Mom was at work or just lying in bed, I would tell myself that I was more independent and responsible than other kids. But as night fell, and I put myself to bed, I felt miserable.

IF YOU DON'T TRUST, HOW CAN YOU
EVER KNOW YOURSELF?

There are several factors behind the isolation that people feel when they grow up living with domestic violence. Families isolate themselves for fear of the consequences; they hide the abuse to protect the family structure, despite its dysfunction. At an individual level, children are often emotionally overwhelmed by what they've experienced, so they are often socially challenged. The stress of witnessing the violence damages a child's capacity to adapt, causing emotional trauma and extremes of social behavior—withdrawal or aggressiveness—that become core dimensions of that child's character.

Research studies show that children who grow up living with domestic violence are regularly ranked by their peers as among the least popular in class.[3] These children often reach the same conclusions about themselves as their classmates: They decide they're socially incompetent. They keep to themselves or they act out aggressively and inappropriately to get attention, because they think that's how life works. As a consequence, they are often isolated from others by teachers, counselors, and other adults.

Daniel Schechter, a professor of psychiatry at Columbia University, has shown that mothers who are in domestically violent relationships tend to misinterpret and misunderstand the emotional needs of their own children.[4] These women often fail to teach important lessons to their kids, which leaves the children socially dysfunctional, to some degree.

Julia was one of six kids whose mother was so emotionally traumatized and overwhelmed that she raised her children in an oppressive, tyrannical fashion. Julia grew up in the Caribbean until they moved to the United States when she was eight.

"I never had a real life when I got to America," she recalls. "My mother was very protective and strict; she got married so young that she never had her own childhood. That was just how it was for women back home. So we could not leave the house. We could only go to school and back.

"My father was an angry man and treated her badly. He was always with other women. When he was home, he would hurt my mother."

As a result of a fire in their Brooklyn apartment building, the family was split across the five boroughs. "My mom and two sisters ended up in a welfare hotel in Manhattan. I had to stay with my oldest brother at my uncle's place in Queens. I felt completely alone.

"Not long after that, on my sixteenth birthday, I went to a party. This was one of the first parties I had ever been to alone. I was allowed to go only because I was with my older sister. While I was there, I met this guy and then, *that was it*. He was freedom for me. He was eighteen and going gambling all the time and running wild, and I wanted to do that. So I left. I just ran away from home."

Her mother pressed charges for kidnapping, and Julia and her boyfriend fled to New Orleans. That's when the abuse began. For two years they lived underground and when Julia turned eighteen they moved back to New York and soon got married.

For the rest of their twenty-year marriage, Julia found herself in the cycle of verbal and physical violence that she'd witnessed as a child. She couldn't leave the house or drive without her husband's permission. She was not allowed to visit her own mother who lived just a block away.

Despite her prison-like conditions, she did her best to maintain the appearances of a normal life. She shared small talk with parents during school pickups, but in reality, she was completely isolated.

It took her husband's increasingly erratic behavior and his purchase of a handgun for her to make the decision to leave, fearing mostly for her children's safety. She filed for divorce and took an apartment, though in retrospect, she says that it was already "much too late. The real damage was already done."

Soon after the divorce, and just as she was starting to rebuild a new life free of violence, Julia's son was stabbed in a fight outside a bodega. At nineteen, he had already shown signs of following his father's example of being violent and abusive to his girlfriends, which is a common theme among men who grew up living with domestic violence. "I know that if I had left my husband earlier, my son would be alive today," Julia reflects sadly.

For months, Julia mourned in almost total isolation. She viewed her son's death as her fault, another failure in an increasingly tragic life. She felt ashamed and alone. But then when her daughter, Grace, came home covered in bruises she realized she wasn't the only one in this situation. At just sixteen, Grace was repeating the pattern with a boyfriend, who hit her when she tried to go out one evening on her own. Seeing her own daughter slipping into a similar depression—a third generation of women in her family who might continue the cycle of guilt, resentfulness, sadness, and isolation—something new surfaced in Julia's spirit, and she found the will to change.

After years of silence and isolation, she began to rebuild her connections with the outside world, talking with her extended family again and reaching out to her neighbors. She surrounded herself with a network of friends and social workers, who provided the sense of stability and security she had always lacked.

Julia already had the equipment she needed to make that transition from alone to trusting. Lacking a meaningful support network in her youth heightened her sense of isolation, a state she became desperate to change as soon as she realized how it was affecting her own child. That loneliness she'd experienced throughout most of her life also taught her to appreciate the value of community and the comfort of being able to share with others. Her hidden strength lay in knowing when to ask for help, and where and how to find it.

She finally understood that she could not continue to live with the lie she had inherited from childhood. She could not survive in a world of isolation, never taking a risk to extend herself and form an emotional connection. She learned to set aside her fears about being hurt or disappointed, and began to embrace the truth that she could place her trust in others. She took small steps toward restoring her faith in people, knowing that, as Ernest Hemingway famously said, "The best way to find out if you can trust somebody is to trust them."

"Now, I feel emotionally protected," she said. "I have a whole group of friends that I can turn to. A lot of them grew up living with domestic violence too. That's something we all have in common. It's hard to relate to other people who haven't been through it. But when you meet someone who grew up like I did, you just know. And that's a real connection."

As a sign of her growing self-confidence, she has gone even further, and took the remarkable step of visiting her son's accused murderer in jail, who himself was a child of domestic violence, to better understand what happened. Julia also began volunteering at the prison, where she started a reading group with inmates and visits every week, offering advice and a nonjudgmental ear for these troubled young men, many of whom also spent their early lives in violent homes. She has not only ended the isolation for herself, she's making it her life's mission to let others facing domestic violence know that they are not alone.

HOW IS THIS PERSON TRYING TO HURT ME?

As both Julia and Eleanor discovered, true transformation occurs when we break through the isolation. It can be hard to expose our feelings when the world has treated us so badly. But by taking small steps to rebuild our trust in others, and assuming their intent is good, we can begin rebuilding a bridge to the outside world.

Of course, the instinct to withdraw is understandable when those you should have been able to trust the most have let you down. Trusting others is a risk. It is more natural for you to assume negative intent. Your first assumption may be that no one understands or that everyone is trying to hurt you. You often overreact. You get upset easily. It feels like you can't control your emotions. So the safest path is to just withdraw from everyone and keep your feelings a secret. But that just makes you feel more alone and misunderstood.

Your suspicions of the motives of others are a survival technique you learned from childhood. It's a pattern imprinted on your brain. It's also a lie that you live every day through the most mundane of human interactions. As Sousa said in our interview:

> When a stranger is approaching you, say someone you're meeting in your line of work whom you know little about, you start making judgments as soon as you see this person walking towards you. The emotional system in your brain goes to work long before your rational system gives a damn, and it's saying, *Look at the*

guy, the way he's walking, his facial expressions. What do you think is behind that face? How is he trying to hurt me? Is this a friend or a foe; competition or a colleague? All these thoughts are running long before the rational brain has had a chance to collect any unbiased facts about this person.

This kind of thinking automatically creates an emotional distance between you and others. Your self-imposed isolation may not even be obvious to the rest of the world as you put up a front and hide that vulnerable inner core. You could be surrounded by people every day and never make a real connection.

KNOWING YOURSELF LEADS TO TRUSTING OTHERS

Trusting yourself is a key to trusting others, but in order to do that, you have to *know* yourself. I don't mean your hunch as to who you are; I mean really understanding your personality—who you truly are. It's not always easy to see beyond the lies, but the latest research in human analytics has helped millions understand themselves. And it will help you too.

In 2009, I took a personality assessment for the first time. I had always thought that these were a waste of time—a diversion with no more validity than the newspaper's daily horoscope. I was trying to figure out what I might do next in my career when a friend suggested a particular online survey that would tell me what I was naturally great at. It was what is known as a personality assessment, and my friend said it was one of the best in the world and was remarkably accurate.

When I read the results, I couldn't believe my eyes. The

description of who I was, was who I wished I could be, not who I believed I was. But I kept reading it. And it got me curious, and increasingly I began to identify with who it said I was. Sometimes, deep down, we have an inkling of our true nature but this assessment gave me a better sense of myself, of what I am capable of. This tool in essence became another One for me. Showing me the truths about me that I could not see for myself.

When you know yourself, you can trust that you have true value. By taking action and reading this book you now already know yourself far better because you understand how your childhood has impacted your life. Only once you know yourself are you then able to trust others.

THE GATEWAY TO TRUST

Indra Nooyi is the CEO of PepsiCo and one of the most powerful executives in the world. A native of Tamil Nadu, India, she has engineered the doubling of profits since she first joined the company in 2000 and is praised throughout the world for her innovative and effective leadership skills.

A friend of mine works for Pepsi, and he was invited to Nooyi's home for dinner with several other executives. He asked her, "What's the greatest lesson you ever learned?"

Without hesitation she replied, "Assume positive intent." Even though it wasn't in her nature to be so trusting she discovered whenever she approached new situations or met new people, accepting that other people's motives were good changed everything. Suddenly her world opened up, and countless opportunities came her way, because she wasn't shutting the door before she could see what was on the other side.

People assume positive intent when they drive a car, otherwise no one would ever take to the road! All that separates you from another is a yellow line. Trusting others is a risk, and so is assuming positive intent. The lie you've lived has conditioned you to avoid the unknown and quickly choose the path that helped you survive. You had to deal with so much risk when you were young, so now you seek the exact opposite and avoid intimacy at every turn for fear of being hurt. Yet the secret to dealing with risk and uncertainty is to recognize it and embrace it. Recognize that you have handled uncertainty when you were a mere child with no security or safety net. As an adult you have so many other resources on which you can rely.

But first, you have to get to know your true nature. You've unconsciously coded so many lies growing up, you can't even trust yourself. Even those who haven't lived with domestic violence struggle with understanding who they are. But you have an extra set of challenges to deal with because you grew up living with domestic violence. As psychology professor Sonja Lyubomirsky explains, "We are better off if we are able to construct a life narrative of how we became who we are today and how our future will unfold."[5]

THE KEYS TO TRUST

As David Sousa told me, trust is "a basic moral value that we have as a society; if you don't have that, you will have a very difficult time reaching your full potential." So you were not trained to trust, you were trained to be alone. Up until now, this has held you back. But that's not who you really are. Taking risks, facing fear and uncertainty, are natural to you. You took many risks to get where you are; you had to—you had no choice. Calculated risk taking is inherent in your nature.

And now you know you are not alone. You never were. There are more than a billion people alive today who grew up living with domestic violence. You are part of a special tribe, a group that, as Alison Gopnik, professor of psychology at the University of California, Berkeley, says, "Owns their past, which allows them to own their future."[6]

You now have compassion for others. All that you have lived through and overcome gives you the potential for an extraordinary level of empathy and understanding. Build your trust in others by giving them a chance. Make others feel appreciated and worthy by asking them questions and listening to their answers. Engage, make eye contact, and cultivate your curiosity about others. Trust in yourself enough to trust in others. All of these small actions will lead to deeper connections.

When you discover your true nature you develop the confidence to assume positive intent. When you do that, you will own your future and never feel alone.

FROM THE LIE TO THE TRUTH

The Lie

You are alone and it was meant to be that way; no one could truly deep down understand or connect with you and that is just as well because they can't be trusted and you will push them away. You had no one else to rely on growing up, so you might as well assume that will always be the case. You may have people around you, but in the end, you will be alone.

The Why

When the people on whom your entire life depends are under attack or behave unpredictably and sometimes cruelly, your emotional world is thrown into chaos, and it's hard to feel safe or to trust anyone.

The Truth

I am trusting. I assume positive intent. With each interaction I have, I assume another's intent is positive. I listen first, without judging.

I know to trust is to take a risk, but I had to take many chances when I was a child, so I am comfortable doing so and have a hidden talent that allows me to take intelligent risks. Trusting someone initially may be threatening but that does not compare to the risks I had to take as a child to get to where I am today.

Now it is easier for me to trust others because now I truly trust myself. I now know myself better than I ever have. I will remind myself of my natural gifts. Now I trust myself fully knowing beyond a shadow of a doubt that I am as worthy as another.

To Try

1. When you interact with others, instead of initially questioning their intent, adopt a mind-set to assume positive intent. Remind yourself, "I assume their intent is positive."

2. Because it takes courage to trust others, remind yourself of the courage you already demonstrated, the risks

you took. The courage it takes to trust another pales in comparison to the courage you displayed early in life.

3. Trust in others comes so much more naturally when you learn to trust yourself. Know what you are good at and what you love to do; this will build trust in yourself.

4. So how are you to know your true nature? Who was there to tell you? Take the survey at cdv.org to learn more and use the code *chapter five* for free access. Your contact information will never be shared. Only you will see the results.

6

ANGRY TO PASSIONATE

When they feel insignificant, they will get angry. The anger gives them a false sense of importance.

—Tony Robbins

Jeremy's grandfather was a highly intelligent man who, according to the Alabama state tests, was a bona fide genius. But in those days, there weren't many opportunities for even a brilliant black man, and all his pent-up frustration and resentment was channeled into emotional cruelty and physical abuse against his family. Jeremy's father, Walter, a Vietnam vet, was also a highly intelligent man who could not seem to make his way in life. He felt held back from the rewards and recognition to which he felt entitled. Jeremy can remember him only in a state of anger that would regularly erupt as verbal or physical abuse.

"My father was kind of a victim and he blamed everyone for everything," Jeremy says. "Even if he was just having a bad day, me or my mother would be the cause of it. He would spend more time being critical of others than focusing on himself."

As a physically underdeveloped four-year-old living with domestic violence, Jeremy did not understand that his father felt out of control and had very low self-esteem. He was unaware of the generations-long cycle of growing up living with domestic violence, exacerbated by racial prejudice and poverty.

As is often the case in homes with domestic violence, Jeremy wasn't the direct recipient of physical violence, but there was plenty of screaming and verbal abuse. What hurt and angered him most was feeling helpless to protect his mother. He keenly felt every kick, punch, and shove she experienced.

In her book, *The Philosophical Baby*, Alison Gopnik says that because children are naturally empathetic that they "literally take on the feelings of others."[1] This is due to the activation of mirror neurons, which cause children to respond strongly to what they see.

One night Jeremy's father turned his violent energy on his little boy with a stream of verbal abuse. But young Jeremy was through with it. He straightened himself up to his full three-foot, two-inch height, stared his father dead in the eye, and said: "You know when I am older I'm going to kill you, don't you?" He was only six years old.

Stunned, Walter said nothing and backed away. The little boy must have convinced him he was serious, because shortly after that his father disappeared out of his life. From age seven, the only contact Jeremy had with him was an annual phone call, when his father would tell him how special Jeremy was.

But Jeremy meant every word of his promise. Ever since that confrontation, Jeremy's singular focus was on getting big and strong enough to beat his father into a state of helpless submission. He wanted that man to feel what his mother felt, what he felt. He couldn't get big enough, fast enough. He took weight gain supplements and trained like a maniac.

"It plagued me," he confesses. "I just wanted to create enough competence to fight and confront and, if necessary, kill this person who I hated from the pit in my stomach."

Jeremy wasn't interested in relationships, he didn't think about building a business or having any kind of compelling future. He was bitter, angry, and guarded, especially when it came to his mother's subsequent boyfriends. He blamed himself that he couldn't defend his mother from his father, something no child should have to do, so he became especially protective of her, to the point that it was next to impossible for her to have another relationship.

BLAME TAKES AWAY YOUR POWER

Jeremy's intense training in his quest to become more physically powerful led him to join the Navy SEALs. This elite and incredibly demanding special forces unit requires an almost superhuman combination of strength, endurance, and intelligence. Tellingly, a recent study of naval cadets suggested that about 48 percent of armed forces recruits are children of domestic violence. All that anger and energy has to be channeled into something, so protecting your country, becoming a uniformed defender, is a logical next step for a person who grew up living with domestic violence.

"The pain of seeing my mother hurt was ten times worse than anything I ever felt going through the SEALs training Hell Week," he says.

With all this training, Jeremy was satisfied with his size and strength because, as he says, "I knew I'd be able to give him a good fight, at least."

But a week before graduating as a SEAL, during a port of call in the Mediterranean, he was called into the chaplain's quarters in the middle of the night and was told that his father had been killed in an accident.

"Thank God!" Jeremy exclaimed aloud. He was so relieved that it wasn't his mother or sister or grandmother. Never for a moment did he think it would be his father, whom he did not consider immediate family.

At first, it was a huge relief, but then it hit him: "I could never be normal. There were all these things I would never get a chance to fix."

Now his long-simmering anger had no outlet. Jeremy would never be able to meet the man and get closure. It was a loss—not the loss of a loved one but the loss of an opportunity, and he felt cheated. More than physical revenge, though, Jeremy was really seeking to understand his own tendency toward rage and how to deal with it. Now he couldn't. This was the truth he had to face. His father was gone, and Jeremy was no longer that puny child, a fact that hit him hard at the funeral and became a turning point.

"Seeing him in the casket, he looked like a scared little boy finally at peace. He looked like me. The moment had finally come, but the anger energy came and had nowhere to go. The energy had to become something else, and we're talking massive amounts of pent-up energy. The only thing it could become in the moment was passion or I would have been buried with him that day."

On some level, Jeremy always knew that his lifelong obsession, and the emotion that fed it, wasn't healthy. Anger in all its manifestations—violence, aggravation, impatience, dominance, controlling tendencies, bitterness, frustration, even the habitual turning a cold shoulder—can become the dominant themes in the lives of people who lived with domestic violence in childhood. These kids grow up feeling insignificant. Their only role models are teaching them that anger is the way to confront most problems. They are misled into believing that acting on anger can somehow give them more certainty, power, and control. While this misconception is understandable, it often leads them to take actions that lead to a life of unrealized dreams, sadness, blame, and unmet potential.

I NEVER HAD CONTROL WHEN I WAS A CHILD; ANGER GIVES ME THAT CONTROL NOW

Anger comes from the amygdala, which is located deep inside the brain. It detects danger and regulates emotional responses to threats, such as fear, anxiety, and anger.[2] It's also responsible for the fight-or-flight reaction we have to danger.

Psychologist Stephen Joseph describes it this way:

> The pupils of the eyes dilate, the heart beats faster, the rate of breathing increases, blood flow increases and is redirected to the muscles for quick movement, the skin becomes cold and pale, fat is made available for energy, hormones surge throughout the body, muscles tense, the bladder empties. Lighter on our feet and equipped with energy that has been diverted from ingestion and reproduction, we are now ready for action. We are ready to fight or take flight.[3]

That threat could be to our physical body or to our inner selves—even to our self-concept. Whether perceived or actual, if someone makes you feel unloved, guilty, worthless, or weak, your sense of self is threatened and that part of your brain will work to find ways to feel secure again.

Both men and women experience anger, although sometimes it comes out in different ways. As Harvard neuropsychiatrist Louann Brizendine puts it, "Once some men's anger ignites, it's hard to stop, because it gets fueled by testosterone. When a woman yells at a man who is angry, he knows she isn't a real threat to him. So her anger just gets him more fired up. His anger is feeding on her anger and then back on his own."[4] For both sexes, anger provides a sense of immediate certainty, dumping chemicals in your body that literally numb the pain.

When children are exposed to anger and violence, they learn to deal with what they perceive to be threats in kind. The brain's job is to keep its owner alive by collecting information, and the data being collected by children of domestic violence during their formative years are the out-of-control, negative emotions of the adults in their lives. By living with violence in their home, they learn that violence is the accepted way to settle arguments. What they see, they do, either to others, or themselves.

According to R. Douglas Fields, "Early childhood experience, such as bullying, abuse, being raised in an unwholesome violent environment, and traumatic events, all affect the propensity for rage and fear. . . . [C]hild abuse and neglect produce long-lasting changes in connections between the left and right brain (corpus callosum), the amygdala (a brain region involved in fear and anxiety) and prefrontal cortex (critical for decision making and complex social interactions)."[5]

Beyond brain and emotional development, the stress of prolonged states of anger can damage the rest of the body. Just consider what happens to the muscles of someone who takes steroids for an extended period of time, and imagine what that does to the body of a developing child. All those feelings, stirred up by a prolonged state of fight or flight, get sustained 24/7 in the life of a child of domestic violence.

REDIRECT ANGER'S ENERGY TOWARD YOUR PASSION

Jeremy really wanted kids of his own someday. But first he had to figure out how to live a life free of the all-consuming desire to avenge his mother and demolish his father. "Rage had become my filter through which I saw the world; my dominant emotion" Jeremy says. "I blamed everyone for everything." Just like his father had done before him.

Because he never wanted to repeat the cycle of violence, he was in a constant state of high alert. By never having the chance to deal with what he now calls his "warped motivation" he knew he had to somehow unlearn what was learned, figure out how to trust, and open himself up to normal relationships. But he didn't know how to live any other way. And the thought that he might be capable of repeating the cycle of violence terrified him.

"I was terribly afraid to have a family or even be serious about someone," he recalls.

Even Jeremy's father's funeral didn't give him an opportunity for closure, and afterward he went into a deep depression. He no longer felt he had a purpose. He tried religion, but none of it made sense to him at the time, so he tried other paths on his search for meaning.

An inquisitive and determined man, Jeremy started reading every personal development book he could get his hands on, doing all he could to develop a self-concept beyond the anger that defined his life. He was determined to learn everything he could about the science of human achievement. He knew he had to change his self-concept. This was key. After a few years of searching, he found a way: He took the energy of his rage, identified it, and then pointed it toward something he desired deeply—to do what he could so that others did not have to experience what he had had to endure.

During his research, he stumbled upon methods to describe how we can turn certain negative emotions into their opposite. Jealousy, for example, becomes empathy. You cannot take away the strength of the emotion but you *can* redirect it. Just as you can't eliminate a habit but can replace a bad habit with one that will benefit you. So he turned his anger to his passion, to an outcome that had great personal meaning. Passion is about immersing ourselves into that which we want most. What we have a deep desire to do, become, experience, or achieve. Fulfilling a passion is a pursuit that transfers the destructive energy of anger into something worthwhile and productive.

Every time he felt the feeling of anger coming on, he would remind himself of the truth—he was not an angry person; this was just a pattern he had learned that can be unlearned—and then would take action toward his desired outcome to free himself of this lie. In particular he took to heart the lesson taught by the influential management expert Albert E. N. Gray, who says: "Successful people have formed the habit of doing things that failures don't like to do. Failures follow their natural likes and dislikes; they are guided by their natural preferences."[6]

In other words, those who don't succeed do whatever they feel like doing, not what they know they must do. Jeremy applied this idea. As psychiatrist Norman Doidge notes, by focusing on something pleasurable in the place of the anger, people can form a new circuit that is gradually reinforced instead of the anger.

WHAT ELSE CAN I ASSUME ABOUT THIS?

Jeremy began this process of finding meaning to the experiences of his life by giving himself the space to recognize and channel all his anger that was just below the surface. When a feeling of anger would come over him, he would ask himself, "What else can I assume about this? What else could it mean?"

Doidge explains that neurons that fire together, wire together: By doing something that is positive, satisfying, and fulfilling, when the feeling of anger strikes, people form a new circuit that gradually takes precedence over the compulsion. By *not* acting on a compulsion the link between the compulsion and the idea is weakened and so is the anxiety that we feel.

"It's like SEAL training. It's all pain, but the experience helps you create a proper meaning for it—pain with purpose." With that statement, Jeremy showed how he had taken control of the meaning of his life. He was able to turn his anger into passion, which allowed him to learn the methods, tools, and strategies that would be needed to help improve the lives of others.

Through an expanded network of like-minded individuals, including many who were also children of domestic violence, he embarked on a career as a local church leader. He also founded a consulting business that helps entrepreneurs and executives reach their true potential. In effect, he discovered a new purpose: to help others.

Gradually, Jeremy's relationships deepened. All that passion—or inversed anger—got channeled into becoming a loving father and husband. Through his work in the community and as a pastor, he focuses on families, helping strengthen them with a particular focus on the spiritual growth of husbands and fathers. In all, he's been a catalyst for change in tens of thousands of lives.

By channeling our energy toward something more than ourselves, we discover our own strength, and our energy comes back to us as a reward. We learn a deeper sense of mastery and control—not over others, but over ourselves—that a momentary impulse of anger can never provide.

Jeremy's example shows how this is possible. You do not have to let anger define you. It's not your truth, just the lie that you learned. You had every reason to be angry, frustrated, and aggressive. You had every right to want to try to obtain some sense of security, control, and certainty because you had none of that as a child.

But what about now? Now that you are an adult? Now you know the truth.

CHANGE THE PATTERN AND QUESTION THE ANGER IN ORDER TO CONTROL IT

Adam, a successful interior designer, is another individual who successfully redirected the energy that his anger created. Sitting today in a café in Carmel, he looks like he never had a care in the world. Though he looks and dresses like a quintessential Californian, Adam grew up in a tough neighborhood just outside of Indianapolis.

Violence between his mother and father makes up his earliest memories. In Adam's case, his mother drove the situation—yelling, instigating, and throwing objects across the room.

"Anger was everywhere where I grew up. And it was especially present in my home," he recalls. "We were actually all pretty emotionally close, especially my sister and mom and I, but there was always this very controlling, confusing mix of love and abuse—guilt, yelling and screaming, physical violence.

"The source of it all was my mother. She was disabled, overweight, and unhappy, so my sister and I were really her caretakers. I hated taking care of my mother because she was such an angry person. And on top of everything else, I didn't dare tell my family that I was gay for the longest time. So I had all this stored up anger and confusion I was carrying around. My father was an alcoholic—very quiet and withdrawn. He could never really stand up to her. None of us could, I guess. So she just ended up walking all over everyone. It all added up to a very bad mix.

"You'd never know from the outside, because my dad took such good care of our house. But during one summer the police were at our place almost every night, called there by the neighbors because of all the screaming and breaking things.

"I grew up hating everyone around me."

Adam was resentful toward other people who he thought were more fortunate than he was. He would often wonder, "Why should they get to grow up in a loving house? They didn't earn it. They don't deserve it." Somewhat delusional, he thought that his anger would cause others pain because they deserved it as much as he did.

Inevitably, Adam's anger spilled out into his life. After he moved out of his parents' house, which he described as the best day of his life, he started drinking heavily and dating abusive partners. He began blacking out during his partying and letting his weekend extend into his week.

"My whole childhood set me up to believe that even if someone treated you like crap—was verbally abusive or hit you—it didn't mean they didn't love you or you shouldn't be with them," he says. "And I was just as abusive right back." At age twenty-seven, after a number of unexplained absences from work, Adam nearly got fired. That was when he asked himself, "What could this cost me?" The fear of losing a job he loved, along with his hunger for financial independence, prompted him to take some dramatic steps: He ended his violent relationship and got his drinking under control, entering six months of rehab.

Through the many relationships he formed in rehab, which he continues to foster, Adam was able to engage with people whom he trusts, to open up about his past, and to help others who grew up living with domestic violence. He gradually forgave himself and his family, although, he admits, "it's an ongoing process." He also realized that he could direct his anger toward working harder at his career. Having a successful career was a way of proving to others that he was neither unimportant nor powerless, that he was not to be ignored. He had discovered the power of transforming his anger into passion.

THE HIGH COST OF ANGER

Acting out, being aggressive, and expressing rage are the natural reflexes for people who grew up living with domestic violence. Manifesting anger is seductive because it creates an illusion of power. In reality, when we allow ourselves to be guided principally by our feelings of anger, we are enabling others to control us.

Finding strategies to control anger helps us channel this energy into much more rewarding and productive pursuits. We discover the truth that we can be far more powerful than we ever realized when we dispense with anger and follow our passion.

But if we don't find some way to redirect that rage, we grow up failing to learn the difference between simply feeling angry and acting on it. "When children fail to internalize this lesson, it has a devastating impact on their lives, because they are acting outside the acceptable norms of society," Sandra Graham-Bermann shared with me in an interview. "The cost is enormous on a personal and a social level. Forty percent of children exposed to domestic violence will develop conduct disorders in their relation to others, and many of them are quickly absorbed into the penal system."

It's worth noting here that children living with domestic violence often become schoolyard bullies. A 2003 study concluded that "exposure to interparental physical violence and direct bullying were significantly associated."[7] And yet bullying has become such a hot-button issue in schools with almost no consideration for one of its primary causes.

WHEN YOU ARE IN CONTROL OF YOUR ANGER, YOU CAN FACE IT

Of course, everyone can at times feel angry. What matters is how you handle that feeling. True passion comes from using your power to control your actions. No feeling of passion is greater or more powerful when you can control the meaning and use anger to move you closer to your full potential. You never have to be a slave to anger when you can transform it into passion. When you take actions that bring you closer to achieving your dreams, you convert anger into passion.

Learning this lesson saved Adam's life, and showed him the truth. He discovered his own passion by immersing himself in his television work. The more he worked, the better he felt, and the more he increased his confidence and competency. His dedication attracted the notice of colleagues and allowed him to build new friendships at work. He began to confide in them, and they helped support his struggles to overcome a difficult childhood. Through his passion for his profession and the feelings of accomplishment from his hard work, the story he told himself changed. Today, he looks on his past with gratitude. He's not mad or sad about it because it made him strong. Instead of it being the reason why he couldn't, he chose to focus his energy on becoming a role model, and now he's mentor to many who share a similar story.

"I can't begin to tell you how different I am as a person," he said. "I am at peace and feel happy. The relationships I have with friends are awesome. More than anything else, the biggest change is that I learned how to manage my anger. I don't argue the way I used to. I can feel when that trigger goes off inside me, and I know that it's time to take a big step back. I try to look at what's bothering me from different angles and not let others control how I feel. In the end, it's me who decides how I react. I control the meaning of what happens to me.

"Figuring that out, and just using those simple exercises for defusing my anger, has let me really focus on me and my career, instead of all that other stuff. I've learned how to get along much better with my mother—she's a difficult person, but I don't let her push my buttons anymore. And here I am today: I've got my own apartment, my own car, a great relationship, and a career I love. It's unbelievable."

TOOLS TO CONTROL ANGER AND IGNITE PASSION

On the face of it, the lives of Adam the interior designer and Jeremy the entrepreneur could not be more different. But their eventual success boils down to the same thing: a moment or a realization that showed them how to turn their anger into something incredibly empowering. Jeremy was able to remind himself of the truth whenever he recognized anger coming on. Adam realized that by asking himself one important question he was able to recognize that his hair-trigger temper and destructive lifestyle was about to cost him his career. Each one of them was able to unlearn what was learned, replacing a lie with a new empowering truth. When they identified the anger and pointed its energy toward a new more productive truth they were able to act in a way that brought them closer to their full potential, enabling them to contribute and improve the lives of others in turn.

"Children witness violence from powerful role models and they learn to manage emotions from those models," Graham-Bermann said. "This is how they learn conflict resolution. They internalize those relationship paradigms and then act out in relation to other people."

But you are not a child anymore. You are in control.

You have developed an awareness of the challenges that you are facing and have acknowledged that you need to take action.

You are learning to understand where your anger comes from. You have come to recognize that what happened to you in your childhood is not your fault and that you have been living with the lies of your guilt, resentfulness, sadness, loneliness, and anger for too long.

You are able to distill the information that you've been gathering through the stories and insights in this book and use it to your advantage. When you have this information, things start to change, and now you have a lot more information, or data, so let's use it. Let's use DATA.

DATA is a simple acronym that provides you with a tool to control anger: decide, ask, truth, act. It is a simple but powerful device to help you focus your feelings, thoughts, and actions whenever you are starting to feel overwhelmed with anger: DATA is a series of simple statements and questions you can ask yourself in the moment that will create space and allow you to look at the situation in a way that puts you in control. This is how it works: When you feel the emotion of anger, immediately . . .

- **Decide** what you're feeling. Recognize and identify anger by asking, "What exactly am I feeling?"

- **Ask** yourself, "What else can I assume about the situation that is causing me to react this way? Could I be mistaken about the true intentions of the person who is making me angry? How would a stranger see it?" Remember, it can take up to six seconds for the rational brain to kick in; the first two steps will help you automatically take the time needed to rationally think through the situation.

- Remind yourself of the bigger **truth**: that you can use the energy of anger and intelligently redirect it toward the pursuit of your passion. You can control only the actions you take and the emotions you focus on. *You can control only the meaning.* Repeat this truth out loud.

- **Act** in a way that moves you closer to your full potential. By simply not acting in anger, you are unlearning what was learned. To simply not act in anger is a significant accomplishment.

FROM THE LIE TO THE TRUTH

The Lie

When someone threatens your sense of self, breaks the rules, or makes you feel not good enough, you can feel important and gain a sense of security by expressing your anger. Because anger gives you control and power, you can use it to let others to think twice about hurting you. You believe that anger is an effective way to solve problems and deal with conflict.

The Why

As a child growing up with domestic violence, you witnessed adults reacting in anger; children often mirror what they see. Unconsciously, you learned that such a response was normal. You often crave security, love, and being made to feel important because those needs were not met when you were young. So now, when you believe they aren't being met, you use anger as a kind of payback, you teach others a lesson with your anger. You use it as a pain reliever. Anger sweeps away everything in its path, overwhelming all other feelings or thoughts and short-circuiting rational thinking.

The Truth

I am passionate. I enjoy working on the things that will help me realize what I most want in life. I pursue my passions.

When I live passionately I take the actions that move me toward my full potential, free from what others think and free from judgment.

I realize that when a thought triggers a feeling of anger, there is great energy produced inside of me. I take control of this energy. Every time I feel overwhelmed with anger, I use DATA and apply it to the pursuit of my passions.

I understand that I cannot control the thoughts and actions of others. But I can exercise the ultimate control—control over the meaning of any situation—control over myself. I am in control of my thoughts and my feelings and my actions, and nothing is more powerful.

I choose to pursue my passions that move me closer to reaching my full potential.

To Try

Use DATA whenever a thought triggers a feeling of anger:

1. **Decide** what you're feeling. Recognize and identify the feeling by asking, "What exactly am I feeling?"

2. **Ask**, "What else can I assume about the situation that is causing me to react this way? Could I be mistaken about the true intentions of the person who is making me angry?"

3. Remember the **truth**: that you can use the energy of anger and redirect it to the pursuit of your passion.

4. **Act** in a way that moves you closer to your full potential by taking that energy and applying it to your passions. By simply not acting in anger, you are unlearning what was learned. To simply not act in anger is a significant accomplishment.

7

HOPELESS TO GUIDED

Because of what they experienced, they can reach a plane that few humans can reach.
— Cloé Madanes, world-renowned innovator and teacher of family and strategic therapy

Born in the 1960s in rural Virginia to a third generation of Irish immigrant coal miners, Annabelle grew up living with domestic violence. Both parents came from a generations-long cycle of alcohol-fueled domestic violence. Most of her family eked out their livings in the coal mines, driving coal and garbage trucks, relieving the poverty with hard liquor every day after work.

Annabelle's father grew up living with domestic violence. Her mother's immediate family of seven siblings (three out of ten had died) lived in a house with no indoor plumbing, so marrying Annabelle's father, a man with a job and the first person who showed an interest, was considered a step up—and a chance to get out of the house.

Annabelle was the eldest surviving child, and the brunt of her parents' anger, frustration, and disappointment. "I caught hell all the time," she recounts, "just for looking at the wrong way."

"I was never allowed to speak and was often told, 'You have nothing to say; you are stupid, dumb, ignorant, ugly, fat . . .'" She wasn't even allowed to sit at the dinner table with the rest of the family.

Her only joy came from playing the organ at church—brief escapes into music that gave her a sense of hope. Annabelle also caught glimpses of what life was like for other people—school friends whose homes were always welcoming, where parents told their children they loved them and everyone sat down at the table together and shared stories about their day. It made her question her own home life, which, "didn't go over too well."

Instead, her parents drummed home a much darker worldview.

"We were always taught in our house to keep running, that life is dog-eat-dog and no one gives a shit about you, so don't you dare care about them," Annabelle recalls. "Our parents believed that you were not a success until you were high on a throne, and nothing else mattered."

Annabelle came to believe the lies that it was a hard, cold world where no one could be trusted, love wasn't for her, and she didn't deserve to be happy. But taking her parents' words to heart, she threw herself into her school studies, so that she could make the grades that would get her into a good school to study a profession that would afford her a means to escape.

"I just wanted to keep going, to survive as best I could."

She eventually made it into a college in Savannah, Georgia. But even then, when she told her father that she was going to study to be a dental hygienist his response was, "Go pick dirt off of people's teeth, because that's all you're good for."

By then, the hope inside that little girl who sang and played the organ in church had been extinguished. Her situation at home had ground her down, and Annabelle was just going through the motions. She was just about to begin her adult life believing it was all hopeless.

Growing up in a violent home is not simply an emotional and physical ordeal—watching our loved ones regularly hurt each other is spiritual torment. Feeling the neglect and rejection of the very people who gave us life is worse than a physical blow. How can we make any sense of so much pain and confusion? How do we give our lives meaning when they're filled with so much suffering?

"Dwelling on negative thoughts and feelings gives rise to a host of unpleasant consequences," explains psychologist Sonja Lyubomirsky. "Those of us who ruminate, self-focus, and worry are relatively more likely to prolong our stress, to feel pessimistic and out of control, to view ourselves disapprovingly, to lack motivation, have trouble concentrating, and are more likely to get stuck while solving our problems."

This sense of futility and overwhelming despair leaves us feeling like we're in a hole so deep we'll never get out. It is called hopelessness.

LIVING THE LIES HER PARENTS TAUGHT HER

Annabelle spent the next few decades of her life on a treadmill, living by her parents' creed to just "keep running." Life became all about those external markers for success—career, marriage, kids, house, money. She got her first degree, qualified as a dental hygienist, and married the son of a wealthy Southern family. Her parents were impressed; she was climbing onto the throne.

But her husband turned out to be a drinker, a liar, and a womanizer who could never hold down a job. For nine years she supported him financially and tried to make the marriage work for the sake of their two sons. On some level, she turned into her mother, initiating fights and being verbally abusive to her husband out of anger and frustration.

When they divorced, her parents couldn't understand. "It must have been you," they told her. Annabelle had moved back in with them temporarily, to get help with the child care while she figured out her next move. But things in their household hadn't changed. If anything, they'd gotten worse. Her father drank heavily, and both parents berated her in front of her children. On one occasion, when Annabelle was heading out to work and called to her kids, "I love you," her father whipped them around and told them, "You don't ever have to listen to that crap again. And you never have to say that to your mother." But the final straw was when her mother started encouraging Annabelle's sons to call her "Mom" instead of "Grandma."

"I hooked up with the first single guy I could find and got out of there," she says.

The second marriage wasn't violent. He stayed home, looked after the kids. For Annabelle, it wasn't great, but it was good enough. She wanted to have more kids, in particular a daughter whom she could raise and love in the way she'd always wanted to be loved, and he gave her that much.

After another nine years, Annabelle tired of having to financially support and care for another man in addition to her four children. On top of everything else, she was working to pay her way through medical school, studying to become a naturopathic physician.

"I did the heavy lifting my whole life and I would have loved to have found someone to take care of me for a change."

FINDING HER PURPOSE WHEN ALL
SEEMED HOPELESS

Instead of waiting for Prince Charming, however, Annabelle started taking care of herself. She got her qualifications, set herself up in a successful practice. She moved to the Midwest, a brand-new market for naturopathy, and set up a thriving practice that charged $350 an hour for her services. She'd established herself enough to become financially successful, with a nice house, four bright, happy kids who loved her, and the respect of her community.

Then a tornado hit the town. Annabelle lost everything—and that sense of hopelessness and despair returned. All the things she believed made up her worth as a human being had been swept away in the wind. Her entire life, she'd lived for acceptance, wanting nothing more than to prove herself and be welcomed by others. She'd talked too much and tried too hard, effectively trying to win over the people she never could—her parents.

But at her lowest point, when all the symbols of her material success were taken away, she finally understood that none of it mattered. Those things were not who she was; they did not define her, because she was much, much more. She realized that she had a deeper purpose. That she was guided toward something more meaningful.

"It took me losing everything to realize I didn't need to be or do all of those things I thought I needed to do. It was all just stuff, and it wasn't working for me anyway."

Annabelle gradually started re-creating herself. "I didn't know who I was anymore." Over the next few years, she reassessed what did and did not work for her; unlearning the things her parents had taught her to believe were the truth.

She simplified her life and moved back to Savannah, the place that had given her a sense of serenity. And today, in her middle years, Annabelle finally understands that her chosen path is about much more than a desire to earn status in her community and have nice things. She now realizes her own value and knows that she's been guided to this point in her life for a higher purpose.

"I am not just a wife, a doctor, a mother, or any of those things. I am a grand soul brought here for a reason—to help others heal."

But Annabelle, whose faith has expanded beyond the strict Catholicism of her childhood, doesn't try to "fix people." She offers love and compassion, to be there for other people, "the way I would have liked people to [have been] there for me." When she sees patients, instead of just prescribing a pill or herb, she looks at their whole life, trying to understand their emotional state and what they need for a greater sense of well-being, combining her faith and humanity along with the science she learned over fourteen years of professional study.

Annabelle's was a long journey, but each experience taught her something and guided her along the path she was meant to travel. She opened herself up to the guidance of others who already experienced what she experienced. She believed that she was guided by something bigger, by the God that she cried out to as a little girl playing the organ. Although her faith had been dimmed over a lifetime of hurt, lies, and disappointment, it was always in her. Contained in her hopelessness were the seeds of hope and faith—her secret weapons—and a determination to find something beyond the domestic violence she lived with as a child.

WHY SHOULD WE BE HOPEFUL?

Hopelessness is a lie that children of domestic violence naturally come to. When we can't control the pain and suffering around us, our expectations are reduced to simply getting through another day. We lose any baseline faith that we live in a fair and predictable world, where there's a chance for a hopeful future.

The lie of hopelessness is further reinforced when we discover how poorly equipped our society is to protect us. For many children, the problem may be so hidden that neither the police, nor the schools, nor social services, nor even the extended family may be able to help. No one ever talks about it. These children then grow into adults feeling that they are truly alone and unprotected in the world.

Under these kinds of circumstances, children fall into a psychological condition called "learned helplessness." Research has shown that the prolonged and repeated exposure to unpredictable and uncontrollable stress conditions will eventually train the mind to relinquish any feeling of control. When we're taught over and over that we can't affect the outcome of a painful experience, our minds expand the lesson to our whole lives—even long after the stress has disappeared. A sense of loss envelopes us, as "giving up" becomes our standard mode of living.

Children growing up under these conditions must contend with a loss of meaning in their lives. In order for people who grew up living with domestic violence to restore a sense of meaning in their lives and feel like they are part of something bigger than themselves, they must reconstruct the story of their life in a way that offers some sense of hope and control. They must find a way to transform their pain into their purpose.

Often that means confiding in someone or finding a role

model—someone who has been in a similar situation and has succeeded in spite of their suffering early in life. Viktor Frankl, the psychologist who wrote the international bestseller *Man's Search for Meaning*, said it best: "In some ways suffering ceases to be suffering at the moment it finds a meaning."[1]

MY PRAYERS WERE NEVER ANSWERED

Believing in one's own progress is important for anyone who grew up living with domestic violence. Because many of the lies that we've been taught are interrelated, each step forward opens up new opportunities to discover new truths. As we start to feel a greater sense of confidence in ourselves and place more trust in the people around us, we can begin to better understand our place in the world. We can place more faith in our own future, and believe—perhaps for the first time—that our life has purpose and meaning.

That's certainly how I felt. I was stuck in a state of despair. I didn't see the possibility of anything beyond the life of survival I was leading, much less a higher power that could guide me toward something greater or give me a sense of a higher purpose.

I carried around this feeling of hopelessness—nothing I did would ever make a difference; that my life was going nowhere.

I couldn't see the real truth because I didn't have enough perspective. I didn't realize that my own courage was carrying me through, and that I would eventually arrive at a place in my life where I could feel safe and be able to help others and feel with absolute certainty that my life has meaning and purpose.

It didn't help that I'd struggled in school. From first through fourth grade, without fail, each year, one of my teachers would

say to me, "Brian, you just aren't that good at [fill in the blank]."
You name it: math, science, penmanship, reading, and so on. In
their eyes, I wasn't measuring up in any of the standard academic
subjects.

When they asked me why I wasn't paying attention, I chose not
to reply with the truth, that I was too preoccupied with fears about
what the night would bring. When they asked me why I didn't do
my homework, I didn't bother to explain to them that I didn't
understand it because I wasn't paying attention, and there was no
one at home to help me. When they asked me why I was fighting
with the other kids, I didn't admit that I thought I was being
threatened, even though as I look back now I see it wasn't true.
When they wanted to know why I never asked for help, I didn't tell
them that I was ashamed to admit that I was letting my mother
get hurt and I wasn't courageous enough to kill the man who was
doing it. I didn't say there is something inherently wrong with me.

So I was told that I just wasn't that smart. And of course the
brain, doing its job, finds evidence to confirm what you believe or
what you are told to believe. After all, my own grades proved it. I
got by on Cs and Ds. It was a foregone conclusion that I was stupid,
so I'd stopped trying. Why bother? I'd already been written off as
a hopeless case, and that was the lie I'd clung to for years.

SCHOOL GRADES DON'T MEASURE OUR
MULTIPLE INTELLIGENCES

This is a common story for those who grew up living with
domestic violence. They are not able to reach their full potential
in school when they are young because they are focused on threats
in the classroom, in the same way that they are focused on them

at home. They can't concentrate. They worry about what others think. They grow up thinking they're not as smart as others, for reasons that have nothing to do with intelligence. I eventually decided that I did not want to end up in jail, so I applied to county college. The good news about county college is that they will take you no matter how bad your grades are. But this time it counted. I had to get good grades or I wouldn't get the interview that would get me the job that would get me the money that would give me the security I wanted so we could finally be safe and I could be important and loved.

So I started researching how to study and came upon work by Howard Gardner, a developmental psychologist and professor of education at Harvard University. In his groundbreaking book *Frames of the Mind: The Theory of Multiple Intelligences*, which is a critique of a notion that there is a single intelligence we are born with that can't be changed, one line in particular struck me: "The score on an intelligence test does predict one's ability to handle school subjects, though it foretells little of success later in life."[2] Gardner went on to describe how we have eight intelligences, but we are measured for only two of them in school. There are people who are naturally brilliant at music and art. Some have a gift for dealing with people. Others have an extraordinary eye for detail. But the mechanism for measuring these other intelligences through our education system is nonexistent. From the first moment I read that passage, my brain began to unlearn the lie that I was simply not intelligent.

Suddenly, I could see that there was more for me than a life of petty crime and disappointment. I had something—a special skill, a possibility to achieve and the means to achieve it. My whole life up until that moment, I never would have guessed that I was intelligent simply because school defined my definition. Being in a state of hopelessness, it was safer to expect the worst, and that was my natural reflex. But that is a lie. The fact is that our gifts and talents often lie hidden, in unexpected areas. And often, our purpose in life can be as surprising as our real abilities.

When we're young, and coming through the pain of living with domestic violence, our lives feel like they're in tatters, and the truth that we are destined for something greater can be hard to see. It's all too easy to feel that loss of faith.

GOOD THINGS DON'T HAPPEN TO PEOPLE LIKE ME

When I met Chelsea Waldroup, she was a lovely young teenager who had found herself in the newspaper headlines. After a long history of domestic violence, her father attacked her mother and murdered her mother's friend. He got thirty-two years with no possibility of parole. It was the end of the violence in Chelsea's family, but the beginning of a long road of healing for Chelsea, her mother, and her siblings.

Raised in the quiet, rural town of Benton, Tennessee, just above the Georgia border, Chelsea speaks in a polite and self-assured voice. She seems to be a typical teenager, with her long, brown hair streaked a punkish, bleach blond, and hazel eyes that nervously sweep the floor when she searches for words to describe her feelings. But that sad smile gives her away, a little weak and turned in at the corners, because she's already seen far too much for her age.

Both of Chelsea's parents, Brad and Penny, were children of domestic violence repeating what they had learned. Although he never laid a hand on his kids, Chelsea witnessed years of her father's violence against her mother, culminating in that fateful night when her father held the whole family hostage at gunpoint.

Until then, their experience of violence in the home was "a part of life," Chelsea explains. "When you're raised this way, you think it's normal."

Chelsea's parents were separated at the time of the incident. About a week before, Chelsea had told her dad that her mother had planned to file for divorce. He told her he'd "take care of it." Chelsea had no idea what that meant at that time, but she later blamed herself.

That fateful day in 2006, her mother, Penny, had gone to Brad's home to drop off Chelsea and the other children. She took her best friend, Leslie, with her because she was afraid to go to that isolated spot alone. She'd even left word with a neighbor to contact the police if she didn't get back by a certain time. After unloading the kids' luggage and a few groceries, Penny and Leslie headed back to the van. Brad told the kids to go inside, and followed Penny to her vehicle, telling her he wanted to discuss their marital problems, but when she refused, Brad's anger quickly turned to murderous rage.

First, he accused Leslie of meddling and then shot her in the back. She died almost immediately. Hearing the gunfire, Chelsea and her younger siblings ran out of the trailer to see what was going on. What they witnessed was a brutal fight between their parents that dragged on for hours and ended with Penny losing consciousness from so much blood loss. The violence only ended when the police and ambulance came in response to the neighbor's 911 call.

Penny's physical and emotional injuries made it impossible for her to stay at her job, and she was out of work for the next twenty-two weeks, forcing her to declare bankruptcy. Unable to cope as she tried to heal, Penny often had to send the kids to stay with friends or relatives.

All the attention, the ensuing difficulties at school, the emotional trauma of constantly reliving that night were all too much for Chelsea, who was just ten years old when the murder happened. In spite of everything, she loved her father. He had been her role model, the one who motivated her to do well in school. And there were many times that she blamed her mother for provoking her father, and for starting all the arguments that led to the violence.

During the trial, Chelsea testified on his behalf, describing herself a "daddy's girl." She was clearly angry at Penny, declaring that her mother had been away from the home a lot and didn't seem to have time for them. "I took his side," Chelsea later explained. Chelsea was in shock for the first few years after her father's arrest and in denial about just how bad it really was. Throughout most of her early teens, she was confused and blamed her mother. She put her guard up, keeping school friends at a distance and withdrawing into herself at home. She didn't fully comprehend what had happened until six years later, in January 2012, when the family was invited to appear on *Dr. Phil*. Hearing the intimate details of her life talked about like that on national television brought it all home to her.

"I was like, whoa! That's my life. It kind of got slapped in my face."

That was when I met Chelsea. I'd appeared on the same show, and we decided to feature Chelsea and her family in a documentary that we were set to produce. Afterward, I invited the family to my home in New Jersey, and I could see how Chelsea was struggling. There was strength in her, a spark, but in the weeks after the show I could see the transition from numbness to anger and despair. Hit by a tidal wave of emotions she'd been holding back all those years, Chelsea went into a depression, driven by the fact that she'd asked to visit her father in prison and he refused to see her. For Chelsea, the anguish, conflict, shame, and trauma added up to proof that her life was hopeless. "I know I am not going to be successful," she wrote to me a few months after she appeared on the show. "Experience has shown me time after time that wonderful things don't happen to people like me."

IDENTIFYING YOUR PURPOSE *FOR NOW*

Chelsea's own turning point, and her discovery of the truth, came as she began to find peers and role models who experienced a very similar upbringing and had managed to achieve success in their lives. This created in her a belief that it was possible, which gave her the faith to persevere when facing obstacles or dealing with temporary failure. She felt that she was being guided by their experiences. For Chelsea, it was a particularly important connection, because it allowed her to feel understood, and more important, it allowed her to see that there were people in this world who had turned their own lives around. Not only did she feel inspired by their experiences but motivated by discovering a purpose for herself.

She found a meaningful purpose for her life—to raise awareness for children who are living or have lived with domestic violence, and it starts at home, with her own siblings. She became fiercely protective of her three younger siblings, and she now considers it her personal responsibility to take care of and teach them: "Family is all we have," she says, "and I want all of us to grow up with more than what we learned as kids."

This purpose extends to her community and beyond. It's a deep sense of her life's mission and the one thing she believes will stay with her no matter what career path she decides to take. Of course, you don't need to decide a purpose for your life that is forever. Your life will evolve. But you must decide on what is your purpose for now, your life's purpose today. Giving back will likely always be part of who she is, but her purpose for now is to ace her senior year of high school and earn scholarships to fund the next phase of her education. A path that she is clearly on.

Meanwhile, she's relishing her role and discovering many hidden talents as both a counselor and public speaker. As she is now in her senior year of high school she's become something of a celebrity in the town where she lives, and friends and acquaintances often remark on how mature she is for her age.

"I'm not your average teen," she admits. "I've been through more than most adults."

Because her story is so publicly known and because she has volunteered to help children of domestic violence around the country, random people of all ages approach her and seek her advice.

"People feel comfortable talking to me, so I get asked for advice by teenagers *and* adults coming from violent homes. They say, 'Oh my god, this kid knows a lot!'"

Chelsea is so poised, so eloquent, that she can stand up in a room of 500 people, share her story, and captivate her audience. "I love to talk, to communicate with others and help." She wants to parlay that gift to help others. "I want to travel as far and wide as I can and spread the word about childhood domestic violence because it's a part of my life. It is me."

Now that she has a sense of purpose, she doesn't view herself as a tragic figure, as someone who is helpless, as she once believed, but rather as someone heroic—someone who overcame the odds through struggle and transformed her pain into something more powerful. Viewing the events in her life in a positive light restored a deeper sense of faith to her life. She now believes that her mother was saved for a reason and that her own survival proved she was being guided toward a higher purpose.

Today, at seventeen, Chelsea's sad smile has broadened into a confident grin. Externally, her family's circumstances haven't changed much. They still struggle financially. Their house is still covered in makeshift construction materials. And Chelsea needs to work her job as a cashier throughout the school year if she wants any spending money. Life is still hard, but Chelsea knows it's nothing compared with what she's already overcome. She feels as if she is destined for something greater, and knows her life is rich with possibilities.

She and her mother have never been closer. Now that she's processed what happened, Chelsea recognized and respects Penny's strength. Chelsea has even made peace with the fact that her father won't accept a visit from her in jail.

"I never got an explanation and it makes no sense," she says, "I opened up the gate and he did not walk through. That is not my fault."

In fact, over the past two years, Chelsea has come to terms with painful issues it can take some adults a lifetime of therapy to sort through. "As I've gotten older I have counseled myself through everything and accepted the fact that it's not Mom's fault, and it's not Dad's fault," she says, with a maturity beyond her years. "Both parents were just part of the cycle."

Chelsea now sees the possibility of a happy life, and firmly believes that she will be a success at anything she chooses to do. "I used to look at myself in such a negative way," Chelsea says. "But now I realize I am going to go somewhere in life. Anything I want to do, I can do. I'm getting ready to really start my life and jump into everything. I've done all the preparation; I have the right mind-set. Now it's all about the action."

POST-TRAUMATIC STRESS . . . HOW ABOUT POST-TRAUMATIC GROWTH?

Chelsea's experience, and her remarkable turnaround, is a real-life demonstration of recent discoveries within the growing field of post-traumatic growth, in which survivors of deeply disturbing events show a remarkable and profound sense of new meaning and faith in their lives, emerging stronger as a result of adversity.

As psychologist Stephen Joseph, author of *What Doesn't Kill Us*, puts it, "post-traumatic stress is a natural and normal process of adaption to adversity that marks the beginning of a transformative journey."[3] Whereas before we may have written ourselves off, believing that because of what we experienced we can't, the new science confirms that it's actually the opposite. Because of what we experienced, we uniquely can!

We have the strength, the insight, and the ability to rebound without years of therapy or pills. It's possible to tap into that potential, and for many who do, the turnaround can happen in an instant.

As Nobel Prize–winning psychologist Daniel Kahneman notes, "Once you adopt a new view of the world, you immediately lose much of your ability to recall what you used to believe or how you felt about it."[4] All it takes is an instant, a moment of sharing your experiences with another, an insight from the One who comes into your life and helps you see things in a whole new way, a life-changing event, or even a single line from a book to shift your whole perspective. Remember what Renee McDonald said in the preface of the book: "Even a small change in perspective can transform a life."

Both Annabelle and Chelsea were able to turn their painful experiences into gifts. Chelsea has language and interpersonal skills in abundance, while Annabelle's intuition and empathy enables her to communicate with those she's trying to help on a level beyond words. The ability to do and be something great was there inside them all along.

BECOME YOUR OWN GUARDIAN ANGEL

As a kid, I used to love watching that Jimmy Stewart film *It's a Wonderful Life*. At night I would think about what it would be like if I had a guardian angel—someone who would come down to me like Clarence the angel did for George in that film. He would visit me from heaven and say: "Now Brian, we have big plans for you up there. But I have an important question for you. While I know you will be busy here on Earth, when your life is over you will come back to us. And when you do, we are going to ask if you fulfilled your purpose while you were on Earth. You may ask, 'What is my purpose?' That is what we will decide right now. While Earth is a wonderful place, we still face many challenges. Is there one challenge in particular that you would like to work on? What problem would you like to help solve? Whose life would you like to make better? How would you like to contribute?"

From the age of seven to my teenage years, my answer was always the same—to have enough so that I could help my family live the life they were meant to lead and to help others so they don't have to go through the same things that we did.

You don't need Clarence the angel to tell you how to decide on a purpose for your life. Whether it was to get through the night or stop the violence from happening, you know what it feels like to want something with every ounce of your being. You are resilient because you had to be in order to survive. The proof is in the fact that you are still here. You are alive on this very day, reading these words. You are present. Now is your time.

FROM THE LIE TO THE TRUTH

The Lie

Life is hopeless, and it will never get better. There isn't anything you can do to make it better, so you might as well not even try. Good things don't happen to people like you. You know it's a dark, cruel world, and in the end that's all there is.

The Why

Hopelessness is a common feeling for many who've grown up with domestic violence. When there is no certainty or security, there is no hope. When you can't control the pain and suffering around you, your expectations are reduced to simply getting through another day. You lose any baseline faith that you live in a fair and predictable world, where there's a chance for a better future. It's safer to expect the worst because it always ends up that way.

The Truth

I am guided.

When I was young, I had a purpose—to get out of that environment—and I achieved it. I achieved the most important purpose of my life at the time. Because of that, I have the means to realize my purpose in life now. I am inspired by the success of others who have come before me who grew up living with domestic violence and whose experiences I use as lessons to help me fulfill my own potential. I am not alone.

I am guided by something more than myself.

Now, I turn my attention to making daily progress toward my true life's purpose, whatever I choose that to be.

To Try

1. The purpose of your life will evolve over time. But right now, ask yourself, What feels right today? It does not have to be a purpose that stays with you forever; don't put that kind of pressure on yourself. It can be your purpose for now.

2. Ask yourself the following questions:

   - What problem (in my family, my community, the world) would I like to help solve?
   - What dreams do I have for my life?
   - For me, what is life about? What is my driving desire?
   - What would I like to have, experience, or give during my lifetime?
   - Whose life or lives do I want to make better?

3. Jot down some quick answers, whatever comes to mind first. Remembering that your purpose will change as you change and grow, what is the purpose of your life for now?

4. Write it down. "My purpose in life for now is to

_____

_____

_____

_____."

8

WORTHLESS TO ACCOMPLISHED

*They desperately need the approval of others to replace
the genuine lack of esteem they feel for themselves.*
—Renee McDonald, PhD, Associate Dean,
Southern Methodist University

Even at the beginning of our interview for this book, Caroline felt
the need to apologize. Sharing her life's story is one of the greatest gifts she can give to others living in her situation, yet somehow
she was worried that her story might not be good enough.

"I feel weird about this, like I don't belong because my story
wasn't nearly as horrible as everyone else's."

The Washington State–based mother of four apologizes a lot,
to everyone, even when there is no apparent reason to. She
believes that she is so worthless that even her pain isn't good
enough. While it's true that she lived with mostly nonphysical
violence, it doesn't make her story any less relevant. Quite the
opposite. She represents hundreds of millions of men, women,
and children who have suffered similar upbringings and feel that
they are somehow worth less than others; that they are not good
enough—and never will be.

"Nonphysical violence or emotional abuse can be just as damaging and more long term, but physical violence is so much easier to grasp. People are more sympathetic," she says. Caroline makes a great point.

As a daughter, wife, and mother, Caroline has spent her life doing for others first and putting her own needs last because it simply never occurred to her that she deserved to make herself a priority. So the lie she struggles with most is a feeling of intrinsic worthlessness—of being worth *less* than others. She has felt powerless and insignificant, has suffered from low self-esteem, and has constantly sought the approval of others. According to research, this sense of worthlessness is one of the most pervasive feelings among anyone who grew up living with domestic violence in childhood and one of the most lingering and damaging of the lies. Without a sense of worth, children of domestic violence lose their personal resolve and often give up on the dreams that nourish and sustain them. Rediscovering the truth and restoring that sense of worth is the foundation of the natural esteem they should genuinely have for themselves. Achievement, however small and incremental, brings confidence, allowing you to build from strength to strength.

WHY WE FEEL WORTH *LESS*

We all suffer from bouts of low self-esteem now and then as we make our way through school, relationships, and careers. Even children from nonviolent backgrounds experience occasional low self-esteem and need to remind themselves that they are good enough. But for people who grew up living with domestic violence, feeling worthless is a constant theme in their lives that can last long into adulthood.

As brain expert David Sousa describes it, "The cognitive belief system is the result of all the information we've collected from the world around us. It's our belief of how the world works and where we fit in. Of course, [even as adults] people who have grown up in a violent home form a different view of how the world works than people who grew up in loving homes. One of our weaknesses as a species is that when we establish our self-concept as children, it tends to stay with us."

In Caroline's case, it all started when she was a little girl in North Carolina, where the entire family had to walk on eggshells to avoid the next explosion of nonphysical violence in her house. To a young child, the choice of words and tone can strike just like a physical blow. There was no physical violence, but fear dominated her life. Her desire to please and the compulsion to be the perfect daughter drove her. It was Caroline's way of keeping the peace in a volatile environment.

Caroline's parents divorced when she was five, and she was heartbroken when her father left. At first, she saw him every other weekend, but the contact became less and less frequent. He moved five states away, and Caroline's mother didn't exactly encourage visitation.

Her mother remarried when Caroline was six; four years later, her stepfather and mother convinced her to sign papers to allow her stepfather to legally adopt her. She was told she'd still be able to see her dad, but as soon as the adoption was official, he no longer had any legal right to see her.

Caroline was confused as to why she could never see him. Nothing was explained to her, and it left her feeling like she wasn't worth fighting for, that she wasn't important enough somehow. Several years later she found a way to contact her father, but when her mother discovered their correspondence she showed one of the letters to the stepfather.

"I have something to tell you," she told Caroline as she brought her up to their bedroom, where the walls were full of fist-size holes—evidence of her stepfather's reaction when he saw the letter.

"It wasn't directly said," recounts Caroline, "but my mother's message was clear: *This will happen to me if I ever contact my birth father again. It was my fault, and I'd better behave myself.*"

It was control by intimidation, another form of nonphysical violence that can have a profound and lasting impact on a child.

I AM NOT GOOD ENOUGH

A farm boy from the Midwest and a former military man, Caroline's stepfather wanted to erase any trace of his wife's past life. He was the father now. Her mom had to keep the house in perfect order and Caroline and her siblings had to do well in school, toe the line at home, and do nothing to challenge their stepfather's authority.

Caroline's stepfather grew up living with domestic violence. A middle child who'd had much less financial success than his siblings, he'd been made to feel that he wasn't accomplished enough. In fact, when a venture with one of his brothers went bankrupt, he felt like a failure. He felt insignificant, worthless. And one thing is absolute: We always find a way to feel important, somehow. And he found it in his home.

By the time Caroline turned thirteen, the nonphysical violence in the home was getting worse.

Yet her stepfather was a good provider, someone financially stable who would never cheat, and who gave the family a comfortable middle-class existence. Her mother never wanted to go back to the life of poverty with her first husband.

Caroline also played her part, excelling in school and college, where she earned a degree in computer science, not that she ever received a shred of affection for her model behavior. Being the perfect daughter didn't bring her much happiness. In fact, she was desperately lonely.

"I always had to have a man on my arm," Caroline confessed. "It was a kind of validation," she says. From the age of eighteen to twenty-four, she was a serial dater, always having another boyfriend lined up before the previous romance ran its course. None of them ever worked out. She never had a clear vision of what she wanted. She dated at least twenty guys until she settled on one— a man very much like her stepfather: stable job, steady, *and* controlling. But he had something in common with Caroline as well: He'd grown up living with domestic violence.

I NEVER ACHIEVE ANY OF MY GOALS, SO WHY SET THEM?

We often invite people into our lives that are like those who have hurt us in the past. As Rick Warren points out, "Many people are driven by their need for approval. They allow the expectations of parents or spouses or children or teachers or friends to control their lives."[1]

It was as if, on an unconscious level, Caroline was seeking to prove she was good enough to her stepfather, that she could make it work.

"Even my mother said, 'He's a lot like your dad. Are you sure you want to marry him?' But like her, I made allowances because I knew he would be a good provider," Caroline explains.

The first few years were fine—well, mostly. It is ironic that the unacceptable can seem OK when you've grown up with domestic violence and your new situation is even marginally better than what you experienced as a child. The early warning signs can just slip by, and be easily explained away, or dismissed.

After Caroline had her first baby, her husband would lock them in the house during the day when he went to work in order to (in his words) "protect her." It continued for years. He wouldn't allow her and their young children to have dinner until he was home, no matter how late he stayed out. Looking back, she now realizes he was just testing her; telling her he'd be home in a few minutes and appearing two hours later to make sure she obeyed his rule.

After ten years, Caroline's husband moved the family across the country to work at his company's headquarters. But his career had a severe setback, which he took out on his family with nasty comments and passive-aggressive behavior designed to put Caroline in her place. One wrong word—something as innocuous as asking for help with the dishes—could result in a silent treatment lasting for weeks, then months, then for as long as a year.

Through his silence, he was effectively saying, "The cold shoulder I give you will teach you a lesson. And I will keep it going until you apologize, and even then I won't easily let it go." But Caroline's husband was perpetuating the cycle of violence from his own family and making things even worse for Caroline and his children in a desperate attempt to exorcise his own pain.

The violence in Caroline's marriage was insidious. She kept making excuses. She told herself things were good enough, for her. She'd do a better job, and it would be better. As unhappy as she was, she was determined to keep the family intact for the sake of the kids. Besides, she was a Christian and didn't believe in divorce. She married for keeps.

The family moved again, to Tennessee, where Caroline's husband decided to start up his own IT business. The mood at home got even tenser. Start-ups can be a white-knuckle ride at the best of times and Caroline's husband had something to prove after the humiliation of being sidelined at his previous job. So the silent treatments grew longer.

Finally, fifteen years into the marriage and the end of one of his cycles of silence, she decided she wasn't going to apologize anymore.

"When you are ready to speak to me, I'll be there for you," she said.

He said nothing at first. They lived separate lives under the same roof. He was working from home, in the basement study, while she was upstairs.

A few days later, he broke his silence.

"When you get in your car today, I hope that you get into a bad accident and die," he told her. His words landed with a sickening thud. But she thought, maybe he didn't really mean it.

A few days later, it was their daughter's prom night. He showed up late and gave his daughter the same cold shoulder he gave his wife. She was devastated, and Caroline was so enraged she decided to say something. It was the first time in their marriage she ever told him off.

Physical violence was the one thing she couldn't accept and when he struck her with his belt and told her to "drop dead," she immediately filed a restraining order and applied for a legal separation. When he crossed the line into physical violence it was her wake-up call—and she knew that she and her children deserved better.

FOCUSING HERSELF ON A CLEAR OUTCOME, NOT A GOAL

Caroline never spoke about what happened, keeping her feelings locked inside. As the children got older and her husband stopped locking his family in the house, she was able to get out more, and developed a wide circle of friends through their church. But she was too embarrassed to open up. But what was she embarrassed about? That as a child she had things unconsciously encoded into her that she couldn't control? Embarrassed that her parents experienced the same thing she did and did not know any better?

At the time Caroline didn't understand that we can counter the lies only by sharing our experiences in order to change the meaning. She does now. For Caroline, who had always found it difficult to share personally, it was easier to write for herself, privately, than to talk to someone about it. As the long silences from her husband stretched from days, to weeks, to months, she decided to write down what she felt. With no one to talk to, she figured this was one way she could start a dialogue, so she started to keep a journal, applying great focus to this task.

The more Caroline wrote the more she enjoyed it. Just as before when she decided that she would never accept physical violence, Caroline exercised the same determination to get down on paper everything that she had felt and experienced throughout her lifetime. Eventually she put some of her writings together and self-published a book, *A Journey Through Emotional Abuse: From Bondage to Freedom*, that she felt could give a voice to others like her.

Again, it was an act of sharing, or self-expression, that put her on this path to extraordinary accomplishment. Writing was the tool that enabled her to free herself from the lie that she was worthless. In turn it enabled her to talk about her experience with others. Writing became a pathway from feeling worthless to being accomplished.

Caroline grew up in a home in which her basic human needs were not met. But she did not fall victim to what afflicts so many children of domestic violence: She is not dead from suicide, addicted to drugs, in jail, or repeating the pattern of violence. That act of writing and sharing led to changes in Caroline's life. With her newfound independence, she made new friends and joined a new church where she found a man who is "the complete antithesis of my first husband." They started slow, as friends, until his kindness won her over. Today, she tells him everything. He is the close confidant she never had before. Seeing her story through his compassionate eyes also helps her get closer to the truth—that she is *worthy*.

IF I WASN'T WORTH CARING FOR, WHAT GOOD AM I?

Like Caroline, Mort never felt good enough. Born in 1952 and raised in a blue-collar town south of Chicago, he was the baby of the family. No one ever hit him. His father was a big guy with a quick temper, but he adored his youngest son and never laid a hand on him. And yet violence, both physical and nonphysical, surrounded him as he was growing up.

The nonphysical violence in particular was intense, with loud and bitter arguments between his parents erupting regularly over everything from money to housecleaning and disciplining the kids. As it often does, it spilled down toward their children—a hurtful by-product of these homes. Among Mort's most painful memories are the insults and put-downs from his mother. As a boy, she called him "you little schmuck" so often that Mort began to think that was his name. As a teen, he remembers a conversation between his mother and one of her coworkers, a nice lady who took a shine to little Mort.

"That boy of yours is adorable," she told his mother. "And so bright!"

"Him? You gotta be kidding. That kid is worthless."

She was just repeating the cycle. His parents were raised in an orphanage that was like something out of *Oliver Twist*. His mother and father each had a living parent, and the homes they were born into were violent. But what hurt most was being left in that cold and depressing institution because their families couldn't afford to keep them. Mort's mother was so bitter and hurt about being dumped there that she never got over it.

His parents were sweethearts at the orphanage and married young—his mother only sixteen and his father seventeen—just to get out of there. They worked hard, opened a neighborhood general store, and were able to provide for their three children, two boys and a girl, far better than their own families did. But what they couldn't offer was nurturing and affection because they never had it themselves.

"I was a latchkey kid before the term was even invented," says Mort, who survived on dinner out of a can during the week. At a very young age, Mort was left alone for hours at a time as he waited for his parents and siblings to get home from work or school, forced to wear a key around his neck to let himself in the house.

Being on his own in the house, however, was usually preferable to what would happen when his parents finally came home for the day. His father was a serial cheater and his mother was cold, withholding, and hotheaded, and the insults they hurled at each other were painful to hear. But much of their abuse was directed at Mort's older siblings, and even strangers. When a man cut Mort's father off in a parking lot, he followed him, parked the car beside the stranger's, and punched the stunned man as soon as he stepped out of the car.

Mort's older brother, Joe, whom he idolized, bore the brunt of the abuse. On one occasion, after Joe told his mother to drop dead, their father knocked out his two front teeth. A burly young man with a temper as explosive as his father's, Joe emulated in his own life the violence he grew up with. Soon after, after a violent disagreement about money with his father, Joe walked out on his family to join the army.

"My brother was my best friend and he disappeared on me," says Mort, who was thirteen at the time. He felt responsible, as if being a better younger brother might have convinced Joe to stay.

Mort's reaction to the violence of the two male figures in his life was to be the opposite—a gentle, gawky people pleaser who lived to entertain others. Somehow, Mort brought out the best in these two men, who treated Mort with kindness and became his protectors. Because Mort was left on his own so much of the time, any crumb of affection they threw his way lit up his world. And yet he was determined to be nothing like them because he could see and feel the pain they were causing to others.

Deep inside, many adults who've lived with domestic violence as children fear that they will be like their parents, and this fear feeds their low self-esteem. But Mort was determined to be the opposite, as both a husband and father.

As Stephen Joseph writes in his book *What Doesn't Kill Us*, throughout most of human history we have been hunter-gatherers, faced with all kinds of adversity: natural disasters, infectious diseases, and attacks by wild animals. These were the forces shaping the evolution of our species. "Accordingly, we are hardwired to adapt to those stressors: Our anxiety reactions are a legacy of our history. In a sense we are survival machines, programmed to react in ways that help ensure our survival," he says.[2]

To ensure his own survival, Mort became that goofy, affable guy who could defuse any tense situation with a joke and a smile. After college, he used that gift for a stint in stand-up comedy, and eventually leveraged his likeability into a lucrative career as a talent agent. He took steps to become accomplished, despite his mother's prediction. Not that he ever quite viewed it that way.

In his adult relationships, he aimed to please but always felt as if he were coming up short. He married a woman just like his mother—cold and withholding—and never felt good enough. She constantly berated him and questioned why he wasn't more successful.

"I gravitated toward the familiar and married the woman who treated me in a way I thought I deserved."

That fifteen-year relationship was just a continuation of what he experienced growing up. His wife was nonphysically violent. She cheated on him, lied to him, and put him down at every opportunity. Despite the unbearable emotional pain, Mort was under her spell. They broke up briefly when the extent of her infidelity was revealed, but after a few months apart he gave her another chance to disappoint him, which she took. When he finally realized there was no way to repair the relationship, she left him for a man who'd just inherited a lot of money.

The drawn-out death of their marriage sent Mort into a downward spiral. He started drinking heavily, gained seventy pounds, and drove his business into the ground.

But then something happened. During his wife's brief custody of their children he could see the toll that her chronic emotional cruelty and neglect was taking on them. His sweet-natured son, the youngest, never complained, but he withdrew into himself. When his daughter, then in her early teens, acted out against her mother's new boyfriend, her mother threatened to have her institutionalized. That was the turning point. It was at that moment Mort realized he had to intervene and become the One for his kids.

"I had to fix myself fast so I could be there for them; I couldn't allow them to feel as worthless as I did growing up."

BUILDING SELF-WORTH FOR HIS CHILDREN'S SAKE

This newfound strength and resolve led him to quit drinking. He quickly built his business back up to a level where he could provide for his children, got sole custody, and has kept them close ever since. Mort decided that the single most important achievement in his life was to be a father, and the health of his relationship with his son and daughter became paramount. Having experienced what it was like to feel worth *less* growing up and seeing the cold and dismissive way his ex-wife treated their kids, he felt a surge of compassion for his children. As they got older, he started communicating with them more, letting them know about their family history, and how it wasn't their fault.

"Thank God for my kids. The other day I apologized for giving them the same mother I had, and they said, 'Well at least we have you.'"

Today, even in their mid-twenties, his children see him almost every day, or at least talk with him on the phone. "We are unusually tight-knit as a family." When he speaks about them, in just about every conversation, his eyes light up, and he can't contain his joy. Their success and happiness are his proudest accomplishments.

DECIDING ON THE OUTCOMES THAT MATTER MOST

Both Caroline and Mort were proactive. They made it their business to find out what they could do to unlearn the lies from their childhood. Once they started to sense their own value, they gained enough confidence to begin to turn those feelings of worthlessness around. By taking the initiative and taking control, they managed to transform the lie of worthlessness into something true . . . a story of accomplishment.

Each of their stories highlights the importance of deciding on what outcomes are the most important in your life. What do you want to be your reality? Your outcomes. By exercising control over our own lives, through small everyday actions, we can prove to ourselves that we're not worthless. Making daily progress through action toward the things we most want in life.

FROM THE LIE TO THE TRUTH

The Lie

Deep inside you are worthless—literally, worth less than others. If you aren't worth keeping safe, if you aren't important to those who created you, how will anyone else value you? You need the approval and recognition of others to replace the genuine lack of esteem you feel inside. When you don't get it, it makes you feel even worse.

The Why

You established your self-concept, your sense of self, as a child through your cognitive belief system, which was the result of all the information you collected from the world around you. You believe the people who were supposed to be the ones who cared for you the most either did not or were unable to care for you. Thus, if *they* didn't think you were worth protecting and loving, why should *you* feel that way about yourself? You saw other children being treated as though they were valuable, so you blame yourself and subconsciously look for every instance to prove the validity of this lie: that at your core, you are worth less than others.

The Truth

I am accomplished.

I now know what I have overcome. I grew up without having my basic needs met—to feel safe, loved, and important. Yet I am here today. I accomplished something at a time in my life when I shouldn't have been so challenged. I paid that price, but now I get the reward of knowing that there is no obstacle that I will face today that could compare to what I went through as a child and already conquered. I am invincible, unconquerable.

Whenever I doubt that I am good enough, I will remind myself of what I have already overcome and this will trigger me to take immediate action toward the most important outcomes that I want for my life.

To Try

Take the time to answer the following questions. State your answers in the present tense, as though each has already happened. Remember, a goal is a *hope*, an outcome is what *happens*. For example, "I have the loving relationship I always wanted," "I enjoy my work and am making $___ per month," "I control my feelings and they are pleasant most of the time."

"What outcome, if realized, would make the greatest change in my life in the following areas? What do I want most when I think of my . . ."

- career: _____
- children: _____
- family: _____
- finances: _____
- intimate relationship: _____
- friendships: _____
- emotions: _____
- physical health: _____

9

FEARFUL TO CONFIDENT

There is no fear like the fear I have already faced and conquered. I recall that whenever I feel uncertain and from that place is where my confidence comes.

—Chelsea Waldroup, 17

For any child who grows up with domestic violence, fear dominates that young person's view of the world—a worldview that is often carried forward into adulthood.

Whether it's anxiety over meeting someone new, having a job interview, or facing a difficult challenge, fear stops us from doing what we want to do.

As psychiatrist Sonja Lyubomirsky explains, "In a home full of pain, quarreling, or coldness, children are chronically stressed and on guard."[1]

Perhaps you hide, preferring to stay in the shadows or blend into the crowd. You may even act out, becoming aggressive to mask the fear you are feeling deep down inside.

Maybe you walk around with hunched shoulders, bent down

in an unconscious attempt to withdraw into yourself, seeking a sense of security you never felt when you were young.

Many children of domestic violence, "prefer the certainty of misery rather than the misery of uncertainty," says child trauma expert Bruce Perry.[2]

Whatever forms this lie takes, know that it comes from living with that visceral fear you experienced as a child. That feeling of terror, and the underlying childhood trauma behind it, feeds the lie that children of domestic violence believe: that deep down they are fearful.

But the truth is that, as someone who grew up living with domestic violence as a child, you are among the bravest—a member of a group of courageous people who have survived difficulties that most people will never face.

Brené Brown, research professor at the University of Houston Graduate College of Social Work, points out that the root word for "courage" is *cor*, which is Latin for "heart." "In one of its earliest forms, the word *courage* had a very different definition than it does today. Courage originally meant to speak one's mind by telling all one's heart."[3] Instead of referring to the heroics we associate with courage today, this earlier definition is about being brave enough to own our stories and *telling the truth about who we are*. Or, to use another word, confidence.

To realize that truth for yourself, however, you must face your fears as they come and be confident in the knowledge that you have dealt with far worse. You can increase your awareness of the inner courage that has always guided you, whether you realized it or not.

GROWING UP WITH DOMESTIC VIOLENCE MEANT YOU GREW UP LIVING IN FEAR

As a child who lived with domestic violence, Olivia knows what it was like to fear for her survival, or the survival of a loved one. Her story begins with the transcript of a 911 call that opens the documentary that I produced, *The Children Next Door*:

911 Dispatch: 11/21/1990 22:13 San Diego, California
(Abridged Version)

Dispatcher: *What's your standing emergency?*

Olivia: *[crying] My mommy and daddy are having a fight. [screaming in the background] . . . Stop it! . . . Don't hurt the baby! . . . Could you just send the police please?*

D: *OK, we're gonna be there. . . . Let me talk to your . . . where's your mom?*

O: *What?*

D: *What's going on?*

O: *They're having some fighting because this has been going on forever and ever. . . .*

D: *How's he hurting her?*

O: *He made some red marks on Mommy's neck.*

D: *Where did he make the red marks on her neck?*

O: *Momma, don't . . . the police are coming. Mommy . . .*

Two years, and at least a half dozen more 911 calls later, Olivia stepped off her school bus and let herself in to the house with the key that they kept beneath the potted cactus on the front steps. She found her mother lying unconscious on the kitchen floor with a large bruise on her forehead. Her stepfather was nowhere to be found. Olivia was quick enough to get help from the neighbors and call an ambulance, saving her mother's life, but she never really recovered from the shock.

For weeks, Olivia refused to attend school or even part from her mother's side. She followed her everywhere, even into the bathroom, and slept in the same bed. Olivia was seeing the world through a lens of fear and retreated from any hint of danger.

Scientists and pediatricians have long observed that overexposure to constant stress creates a state of hypervigilance in children, but recent studies have helped explain exactly why. As detailed by Harvard University's Jack Shonkoff, the conditioning effects of fear and stress actually alter a child's brain architecture. Chronic stress exposure puts the part of the brain that detects danger, the amygdala, on permanent alert. As a result, all incoming stimuli, whether a siren, the phone ringing, or a stranger's arrival, are easily mistaken for a threat. Fear becomes the default response to everything.

As brain expert David Sousa explained to me in a recent interview:

> This puts children at a terrible disadvantage. They're constantly evaluating potential threats, so their brains get stuck in survival mode, without any time or energy left over to actually *thrive*. Instead of channeling their attention towards learning and building their advanced cognitive skills or social interactions, exercising that developing part of the brain called the neocortex, they prefer to withdraw. They carry this extra burden

throughout the day; they have to know they're safe in
order to learn—but they can never really feel safe.

Even today, at twenty-nine years old and the mother of a son
and daughter, Olivia still struggles with fear in all its manifestations. "Every aspect of life I've lived through the filter of pain and
paranoia," she says. "Something I acquired from being afraid all
the time."

It's a common theme for many who've lived with domestic violence. As Rick Warren points out, "Regardless of the cause, fear-
driven people often miss great opportunities because they are
afraid to venture out."[4]

I RESCUE YOU ONE NIGHT, YOU HURT ME THE NEXT

As is often the case for those who grew up living with domestic
violence, no one on the outside could have guessed Olivia's circumstance. Her family lived on a quiet, middle-class street in
Rhode Island. A family snapshot shows seven-year-old Olivia, wearing pink sunglasses, and her younger sister, just three years old,
playing in a small Little Mermaid wading pool on the driveway of
their colonial house. It's hard to reconcile that adorable smile
with the call that was recorded by the local police a few weeks
later.

"People are just terrified by that tape, but it was just one of
many like it in childhood," says Olivia. "It was my life, on a daily
and weekly basis, and what's been recorded is not even my worst
childhood memory."

Her mother was typical of many women who have babies when

they are still just children themselves. Olivia never met her birth father and instead endured a series of men who cycled in and out of her mother's life. Olivia was hit too but, as is often the case, it was the physical violence and verbal abuse against her mother that hurt her most.

As a child, Olivia's role would alternate from savior—the supportive eldest child who comforted her mother after the latest outburst of violence from a boyfriend—to an inconvenient presence just two or three days later. The insanity of having to keep peace between these two adults "pretending not to see the elephant in the room" was like torture, Olivia confesses, but nothing was as painful as the fact that the woman who was supposed to be her protector "always picked him. That's what haunts me most."

After the police became involved in a few more incidents, Olivia spent part of her childhood at her grandmother's house, dividing her time between that quiet suburban home with strict rules on behavior, and her mother's apartment, which had become a kind of "urban ghetto gang environment" on the poor side of town.

This dual existence took its toll on Olivia's education. Shy, withdrawn, and constantly on edge, she was bullied in elementary school, which is common for children like her. She didn't play much with other kids her age. They often called her names, sensing as children do that she was different and vulnerable. She had so much trouble concentrating that her teachers became exasperated, wondering why she could not do the simplest work. When she got back to her grandparent's home, there was even less sympathy.

The negative feedback was unrelenting. "As a kid, you just end up thinking the world is so horrible."

She flunked eighth grade and "screwed around" so much her second time around that her teacher finally asked why she bothered to come to school. "Because," Olivia replied, "my mom calls the police if I don't leave the house."

The teacher, anxious to move Olivia through the system, gave her some books and reports to write up and then passed her. Olivia was always bright and articulate; there were just certain roadblocks she couldn't get past, and no one to help her at a time when it could have made all the difference.

High school was worse. The anxiety-ridden teen had many social phobias and was especially wary of boys. She begged to go to the same school as the rest of her friends, but Olivia's mother refused, insisting it was in a bad neighborhood.

"I spent my teenage years on the streets during the day, then going back to a very violent home during the night."

"Even when I was sixteen, I knew there's no possible way to build a life when you don't have a platform, an education, or a family," Olivia recalls.

She never went back to high school; instead, like so many people who grew up under the shadow of domestic violence, she played out the cycle, reliving her worst fears and memories by moving in with a man whom she believed would take her away from the violence. He was no different from her mother's abusive boyfriends, and yet Olivia stayed, even as the violence got worse.

She felt trapped because she was totally financially dependent on her boyfriend. But something inside her told her there had to be more.

"By the time I was nineteen, it felt like my friends were moving on and doing great things with their lives," she explained, "but I just felt like the weight of my traumatized past was bearing down on me. I needed to be a part of something. I was tired of feeling like I had nothing."

TAKE ACTION EVEN WHEN FEAR HOLDS YOU BACK

One day, she opened up to one of her few close friends. "I was telling her about that 911 call I made that saved my mom, and how I knew that someday, if I stayed with my boyfriend, this was going to happen to me," Olivia recalls. "My friend said something like, 'I could never have done what you did. To be six years old like that and call the ambulance and take your mother to the hospital and take care of her. You've got more guts than anyone I know.'" That casual observation gave Olivia an opening to look at herself differently. It was a moment when someone came into her life, and a simple act of sharing helped Olivia awaken to the truth: In spite of the fear she had showed not only a deep and abiding resiliency but also an incredible amount of courage for one so young. As Lyubomirsky points out, "Having a history of enduring devastating moments toughens us up and makes us better prepared to manage later challenges and traumas big and small."[5]

"Hearing my friend's words—that I was stronger than I realized—made me start thinking about what was really possible in my life, that deep inside I was courageous and confident," said Olivia. "It actually changed my point of view on who I really was. It didn't take away the fear, it didn't take away any of the problems, Lord knows. But I saw myself differently. It's like I became someone new at that moment."

After a lifetime of hurt, it can take a while for awareness to lead to action. Often fear will stop us. Olivia discovered that she could address and deal with any fear that presented it to her as an adult because it paled by comparison to what she had already faced and overcome as a child.

By the time Olivia's second child was born, she was determined not to follow in the footsteps of her own mother. She didn't want her children growing up living with the violence she'd experienced as a child. And for the first time in her life, she asked for help.

She turned to a woman who'd reached out to her after hearing the 911 tape, which the police had released to help train officers and raise awareness about the effects on children who live with domestic violence. This woman had tracked Olivia down and helped her to get the resources she needed.

Olivia spent the next several months staying in shelters until she could get on her feet. The circumstances weren't ideal, but by then she'd developed enough of a network that at least she had plenty of support and protection. Financially, it took her a while to get established, but there was no way she was going to put up with the violence she'd lived with for so long.

"I want to be around for my kids and give them a good life. I now know that I've got it in me to fight for that."

CONFIDENCE GROWS WHEN YOU KNOW YOU'RE NOT ALONE

What required the most confidence for Olivia was asking others for help—the same confidence it took for her to call 911 when she was that frightened little girl. In the past she put walls up and was suspicious of everyone's motives, fearing more hurt, disappointment, and rejection. But then her preparedness instinct kicked in.

Olivia's greatest desire is to give herself and her children a safe home—a better life. By honing her survival instincts, a powerful by-product of living with fear for so many years, she got past her fear and found the confidence to get them out of a situation that could have destroyed this dream. However paralyzing fear can sometimes be, it can also give you the confidence to prepare and to clearly see the outcomes for your life that you most want.

Once she began opening up and sharing her story, Olivia received overwhelming support. She's been raising her daughters, working various part-time jobs, taking classes at a community college, and working toward her GED. Olivia discovered she's great at sales, communicates well, and has an aptitude for business, although she knows she has more work to do to reach her most important outcome of financial independence. It's not been one single breakthrough so much as it's been daily progress toward that which she most wants.

"In the past, I always felt broken in some way. I felt like I could go only so far before I'd be defeated by the onset of some memory, and I was always afraid. What I didn't see was that the same strength that let me get through my childhood could help me overcome my fears. It was possible to beat my past before it could beat me."

Olivia began to recognize that many of her actions and feelings such as her low-level anxiety, a slightly cynical, suspicious nature, a fear of failure, jumpiness, mood swings, avoidance of confrontation, even an inability to show affection without reservation—all of this was tied to the lie that she learned. That she is fearful. And while the lie of fear may affect everything we do, we put up a brave front. We keep that fearfulness well hidden, even to ourselves.

WHY DO I HESITATE? WHY AM I UNCERTAIN?

There are no visible scars on Payton. No one could imagine what she's lived with most of her life. This stunning twenty-three-year-old Idaho native is literally a beauty queen. She walks tall and proud in front of thousands of people on the Miss America pageant circuit, sings, gives speeches, and throws herself into her work mentoring other young women and girls.

But the reality is that she has never felt truly safe. A sudden noise, an innocent hand gesture too close to her face, anything that even remotely echoes the violence of her past can cause her to flinch, and send her heart racing. She suffers all the classic symptoms of post-traumatic stress disorder (PTSD), just like a military veteran who's seen combat.

And that's exactly what her childhood was: a combat zone. Payton's mother, who had grown up with domestic violence herself, was only a teen when her daughter was born. Payton's father left them by the time she was a year old. Her mother soon became pregnant by another man, and gave birth to a son. So by the time the man who would become her stepfather came along, when Payton was about two and a half, her mother didn't believe she could do much better. And that's when the violence started.

To the rest of the world, Payton's childhood must have appeared like a comfortable, middle-class existence. They weren't rich—her stepfather was a supervisor on a cattle ranch—but her mother could afford to stay at home and raise her kids. Outwardly, they were devout Christians, with a wide circle of like-minded family friends.

But behind closed doors, it was a starkly different picture. Anything could trigger the violence. Her earliest memories are of her mother screaming. "It got ugly really fast." Her stepfather physically abused Payton and her brother, but it was the violence between him and her mother that made her the most fearful.

"When you're little you don't know, you're just so scared," she says. "I would always panic and didn't know what to do, I was so uncertain."

They had another child, and her mother continued to defend her husband to her children. Payton's mother would put makeup on her daughter to hide the bruises when she went to school. When the bruises were too bad to hide, her parents would phone in and say she was sick. At the time, Payton didn't even know it was wrong, because she had nothing else to compare it to.

As she got older, she became more aware of how the world works, and started asking questions, so her mother lied some more. "She used to say that if we ever told we'd be sent into foster care, we'd get separated, and I could be really hurt or molested," Payton recalls, although she found it hard to imagine anything worse than the life she was already living.

As Payton got older and stronger, she started fighting back. Normally outgoing and social with friends, no one in her high school knew what was going on. But it reached the point at which she withdrew from people, cut classes, and her grades suffered. This triggered more violence at home because, "my stepfather expected all of us to be perfect."

When Payton was sixteen things really escalated. One day, as her stepfather was being verbally abusive, she turned and walked away. As she headed up the stairs to her room, he grabbed her by the hair and started hitting her in the head.

Later that day, her head still throbbing, she decided to see a counselor at school, who immediately sent her to the hospital where they checked her out and admitted her for the night. It gave her time away to think about what she wanted most in her life. This moment in the hospital was a moment of peace and she was able to reflect on her future. "I was so tired of feeling this way, physically and emotionally," she says, "I was sick of the pain, and the fact that I never had my mother's protection."

Payton figured that the best way out was to get into a college far away from home. She applied for scholarships and worked on her grades. Her instinct told her identifying an outcome, seeing it clearly, and taking steps to prepare for it to happen would get her what she most wanted.

She got accepted at a college in Arizona, and at first everything was going well. But even in this safe haven, all the fear and panic that she'd experienced as a child caught up with her. She was finally away from home, living in residence at college, but the safety of distance didn't end her pain. Within her first semester at college, she began waking up every night in a cold sweat from nightmares.

She started chugging an over-the-counter sleep aid to help obliterate the dreams, but they kept coming back, triggering panic attacks. It was worse during the school holidays, when all the other students went home and she stayed in her dorm, avoiding family. Without the distraction of classes and the chatter of other people, there was nothing to keep those dark memories away. At one point in her profound exhaustion and constant state of panic, she attempted suicide.

"I know this wasn't normally me and that something was going on here causing me to be like this, but I didn't know who to talk to about it."

In her second year at college, a school doctor told her she was depressed and prescribed an antidepressant and an anxiety medication to keep her sleeping through the night. The doctor never asked her about her past in an attempt to find the source of her emotional state. Masking the problem with drugs only made her feel worse.

The fear was always there, lurking under the surface. So she quit school, feeling hopeless about getting better. Over the next year, she tried a couple other therapeutic programs and pharmaceuticals until she was finally diagnosed with PTSD and was put on more medication to keep her anxiety under control.

―――――――――

With nowhere to go once she'd quit her studies, Payton moved in with her grandmother and things were OK. But the reprieve was only temporary. Her grandmother decided to buy a house together with her parents. And with no income and nowhere else to go, she was forced to live back under the same roof with the people she was trying to escape.

The moment she was back in her stepfather's presence she reverted to her state of paralyzing fear. All he had to do was raise his voice to send her back to that place where she felt like a frightened little girl. Twice in one year the panic attacks became so acute she had to go to the emergency room.

THE KEYS TO CONFIDENCE

In the back of her mind, Payton had the notion that she might be attractive enough to participate in a beauty pageant. And she saw this as a possible way to get out. When she was researching how to get into a pageant, she met a woman who saw her potential and helped her prepare to compete. Sparked by her new friend's confidence, she threw herself into the process. She worked on her singing, signed up for training in public speaking, and even took the lessons on how to walk and hold herself.

"I would get really irrational over small stuff," she says, when she thinks about the effort it took. "I am a people pleaser, and when something was not going right or someone was upset with me, I automatically got nervous again. I always saw myself in a certain way. It was hard for me to accept the compliments. I couldn't even look people in the eye. Even positive feedback scared me. I guess that I thought it could all be taken away so quickly."

The pageant circuit took her out of town and out of state and away from her family, creating more circumstances that allowed her to heal. Instead of hiding out in hotel rooms crippled by fear, she ventured out and introduced herself to some of the other girls and slowly built up a confidence she never knew she had.

Payton, like so many who've grown up with domestic violence, had to get past the lie of fear. She made the decision to change her life and followed through with her plans about what to do at each step, so she was prepared for the obstacles that might have thrown her off course. Because she prepared herself, she was able to be bold. She came to believe in herself and know that it was within her to get what she wanted.

There is new evidence from Harvard that concludes that this preparation can come from simply using your body differently. Professor Amy Cuddy found that when people breathe deeply, lift their chest, move their shoulders back, and keep their head up that this "power pose" actually creates greater confidence and makes it easier to take a step forward when we feel afraid or tentative. Perhaps when a feeling of fear is triggered within us this is our first step, a step of preparation.

Payton used this technique, as for her, the pageant work wasn't just about strutting on a stage. In fact, it led her to find a cause to support, which was part of qualifying for the pageant. She eventually became a very vocal advocate for children of domestic violence, speaking on their behalf at every opportunity, campaigning to give them a voice, and building one-on-one relationships with young girls in shelters who come from these homes.

"I finally saw that it was all connected. A lot of people were in the situations they were in because they grew up living with domestic violence. I wanted to let them know that what they experienced in their past doesn't have to be their future. I was able to clearly see that everything I went through has prepared me for my true calling in life."

Payton had made mistakes, giving in to despair, giving up on herself. She almost let fear crush her dreams and end her life, yet even her doctors couldn't figure out the connection to her past. But she made that leap for herself once she was aware and had the understanding, accepting that the past and present are linked, and now she uses that awareness to help others.

Payton doesn't let her fear stop her. She's no longer afraid to hope and to believe in others. She has the confidence to confide in people and accept their help. She's built up a tight-knit circle of friends at her church who she knows are there for her whenever she needs support. And she met a patient and kind young man who makes her feel secure and who is now her fiancé.

THE FEELING OF FEAR IS OFTEN A SIGN— TO PREPARE

Payton's blossoming into a beauty queen and becoming an advocate for children of domestic violence took a confidence that came to her only after she recognized her own courage. Once Olivia shared with another she was able to see the confidence she always had inside through the eyes of another. Awareness, sharing, and preparedness helped these young women tap their vast inner reserves of strength, so that they could begin to live their lives on their own terms. Their stories reflect a famous maxim from Mark Twain, which defines the truth for all children of domestic violence: "Courage is resistance to fear, mastery of fear, not absence of fear."

Whatever form it takes, fear is that thing that stops you from doing what you desire most, whether it's telling him you love him, believing in yourself, or going on the interview. But it doesn't have to. When you feel fearful it is a reminder that you have to prepare and make real the outcomes that are most important. This preparation and visualization allows us to enjoy these desired outcomes ahead of time and provides us with the confidence to *act as such*, leading us right where we were destined to be.

Further, for you, preparation is natural. When you were a child, you had to think ahead. You watched for the signs and read every subtle cue for the next episode of violence, the next hurtful word, and then you thought through your next move. Planning and preparation is what pulled you through. The more you prepare, the more confident you can become. Growing up, you never got to feel that natural confidence that is in you, because the fear was so real. It was a constant. In your mind, you did prepare, but it didn't stop anything. It didn't work. That's how I felt, well into adulthood. I'd always identified myself as fearful, even cowardly, because I was never able to stop Keith. I was embarrassed that I could allow the violence to happen. I kept asking myself when I was a boy, "How can you allow someone to hurt the woman you love most in life, your mother, the person who created you?" It defies all laws of masculinity; it emasculates a boy before he ever has a chance to become a man. And that lie was the deep, dark secret I'd clung to since childhood, until a random conversation with a stranger on a plane.

It was a flight from L.A., and for some reason I struck up a conversation and let my guard down. The conversation flowed, and he asked some good questions, one of which was, "Who do you admire most?"

I told him that I admire those who are strong and confident and courageous. When he asked me why, I froze. It was my greatest fear. But instead of doing what I would usually do—look down and change the subject—I said, "Because if I was confident, what happened in my home when I was a child wouldn't have happened." Then the next step was easier as I told him the truth, which I had never shared before: "It was because I was not strong, that I lacked courage," I noted, while explaining how I grew up. He looked increasingly shocked as I went on. I thought he was shocked about the story, further solidifying the point in my mind, "How could you not have stopped it?," but he wasn't. He was shocked that I believed what I believed about myself.

"Wow, I don't see it that way," he said. "I couldn't imagine my kids experiencing that for even one night. I can't imagine experiencing that as an adult! But you, you lived through it, you are here. You are courageous. You were scared but came through it anyway. No other fear could compare."

As he said that my eyes welled up. I didn't cry exactly, it was just the type of tear that comes over you on occasion, so that when you blink it washes your eyes and makes everything very clear a moment later.

FROM THE LIE TO THE TRUTH

The Lie

You are fearful. You lack confidence and courage because you were unable to stop the violence you grew up with. You will always be afraid of rejection because you were in some way rejected by those who created you. It's safer to bend down and fit in. You are destined go through life allowing fear and anxiety to hold you back, to stop you from realizing your goals and dreams.

The Why

The conditioning effects of living with fear alter a child's brain architecture. Exposure to chronic stress puts the part of the brain that detects danger on high alert. Fear becomes the default response to everything. You naturally focus on all the bad things that could happen and that thought process stops you from taking action.

The Truth

I am confident. There is a natural confidence and certainty that was conditioned in me from a very early age.

There is no fear that I could potentially face this day that will compare to the fears that I have already faced and overcome.

I recall this simple fact when facing a fear that holds me back from taking action toward my full potential. I am confident. There is nothing that can be thrown at me that I can't handle.

To Try

1. Review your answers to the questions in the "To Try" exercise in Chapter 8.

2. Choose three of the desired outcomes from that list that you want to make progress on in the next three months.

3. Write down three action steps for each outcome that you can take this week, something straightforward for you to do. Something that will build momentum.

4. Write these three outcomes somewhere where you can access them each day.

5. Take three minutes or so each day to say the outcomes aloud and after you do, see them in your mind as if they had already happened. For example, close your eyes and imagine a TV screen in front of you that shows you realizing and living that desired outcome. Think of it as a thirty-second commercial. Let the commercial for each outcome loop a couple of times.

6. Schedule time this week to take the action steps you wrote down.

7. When you know you need to act, but something is holding you back, adopt a power pose and take the first step with confidence.

10

SELF-CONSCIOUS TO ATTRACTIVE

*I'm one of the world's most self-conscious people. I
really have to struggle.* —Marilyn Monroe

Emily looked every inch the part of her cheerleader role in high
school: pretty, bubbly, and naturally slim and athletic. But it was
all a front. She felt anything but attractive and could barely make
herself look in the mirror each day. Not liking what she saw, she
alternated between binge eating and starving herself to the point
that her hair started falling out.

She ate just enough to keep up her performance as a gymnast,
maintain appearances, and remain sharp enough to stay on the
honor roll in school, but she never loosened the tight control over
her diet. It never got to the point at which it was endangering her
life, but it's taken a long-term toll on her overall health and me-
tabolism. Meticulously managing how she looked on the outside
was her way of trying to feel better on the inside, not that it ever
worked.

"I know I'm not hard on the eyes, but when you look at yourself, your whole perception is skewed. You don't see what's there, what other people see. For years I just saw what I thought was there—an ugly little girl who was not loved and didn't deserve to be happy."

No matter what we look like, if we believe we truly are guilty, resentful, sad, alone, angry, hopeless, worthless, fearful and unloved—all the lies we've been discussing in this book—we can't help but feel self-conscious. When your cognitive belief system is flawed, it is not possible to feel physically good enough. That we are fundamentally not attractive is a lie that we carry with us. It stems from growing up with domestic violence. We may try to fight the relentlessly negative inner voice with superficial fixes such as clothing or makeup or trading sex in an attempt to feel wanted. Others find forms of self-destructive behavior to soothe them-selves: overeating, smoking, overdrinking, taking drugs, or lapsing into anorexia or bulimia.

Of course, they don't consciously make the connection be-tween their growing up with domestic violence and why they feel *unattractive*. That fact has simply not been shared with them. They don't stop and say, "I know that I believe I am unloved because my mother and father constantly insult me and therefore I hate myself, and feel physically unappealing." They just *feel* it. And that feeling creates a deep psychic wound. This scar is invisible, but it affects your thoughts and feelings and the actions you take. You feel insecure and self-conscious.

FEELING SELF-CONSCIOUS

Growing up, Emily never felt secure. At five years old, she remem-bers being huddled together with her brother in her bedroom while their parents fought downstairs. Two years her junior, her brother often crept into her bed at night. But something about the arguing this night was different. The screams got progressively louder and ended with an audible smack. Emily's brother ran downstairs to see what was going on while Emily waited frightened upstairs. When her parents saw him the violence stopped but that was the night her parents split. Emily never saw her birth father again while she was growing up.

After the divorce, her father moved away while Emily, her brother and mother had to move to a government-subsidized two-bedroom apartment overrun with cockroaches. After living in a nice suburban neighborhood, the change was a real shock.

Even though their living standards fell, Emily's mother made sure her kids got the best education possible. She took on extra jobs and saved money so her kids could continue their after-school activities. Emily's father had never hit her, and she doesn't recall a long history of violence at home, although her mother "put the fear of our father in us and really freaked us out."

The family was starting to adjust to this new life when a new man came into their lives.

Ted lived down the hall of their apartment building with his parents, even though he was in his late thirties. Emily felt there was something odd about him. Soon, he'd moved in, and it wasn't long before the violence started.

Emily's mother threw him out, but he came back begging for another chance. She asked her kids if she should give it to him. Emily begged her to say no. But her mother took him in again, and so the cycle began.

WE DON'T THINK WE DESERVE ANYTHING MORE

Emily's mother grew up living with domestic violence, and it left her feeling worthless. She did what she thought was best for her children based on what she knew.

Emily's mother felt ugly because she too believed all the lies, and it affected her relationship choices. The brain, as we have learned, encodes sexual reproduction. It encodes sociability, so that you can remain a member of the tribe. We meet members of the opposite sex through an emotional and social connection so that we can procreate, but when we don't feel worthy of love, when we are made to feel unattractive, not only physically but even deep down, we accept partners who reinforce what we learned in those formative years.

This holds particularly true for women and problem solving. According to Louann Brizendine, a neuropsychiatrist and author of *The Male Brain*, we have two emotional systems that work simultaneously—the mirror neuron system (MNS), which is responsible for reading and mirroring emotions of others, emotional empathy, and listening, and the temporal parietal junction system (TPJ), which covers analysis, cognitive emotional processing, cognitive empathy, and problem solving.

"For reasons, that scientists don't yet understand, men switch out of the MNS within seconds of an emotional problem. Women stay in the MNS much longer," Brizendine explains.[1] The end result is women have a greater muscle memory for emotions. They record not only facts and figures but also every detail of the emotion they are feeling. So when women recall fights, for example, they not only remember the facts, but they also reexperience the sadness, anger, and fear all over again. So that ache of sadness and worthlessness, feeling unattractive, and being self-conscious lingers and informs choices. The way Emily's mother was "programmed" to accept such feelings directed the decisions she made about the men in her life, her potential mates. At some unconscious level, she believed she could not do any better.

AS CHILDREN WE HEAR IT ALL

Even though Emily and her brother were rarely hit, her mother had no idea how her choice affected her children. Often when the violence started, Emily and her brother would jump out from their bedroom window on the second floor and run to a nearby park. "I've heard some say in the past that they stayed in the relationship for the children and they thought the children were asleep and didn't hear any of it," says Emily. "Guess what? Children are great at playing possum when in situations like that. We huddle under our blankets with our stuffed animals, shedding silent tears of total anguish. We hear it all, and deep inside we are torn apart by the violence; it changes us forever. I tried to put it in a dark closet somewhere deep in the recesses of my mind, hoping it would eventually go away, but it never did. It eats at me, silently."

Eventually things got to a point at which the violence was so bad that Emily's mother ended the relationship. While the violence stopped, what remained was a profound sadness, which Emily's mom tried to relieve through alcohol. The family was then living on a welfare allowance that was supplemented with her mother's income as a crossing guard. There wasn't enough to eat, and Emily had to suffer the taunts of other kids because poverty forced her to wear the same clothes to school five days in a row.

It reinforced that self-conscious feeling and fed those impulses that led to her eating disorder, but it also made her more determined to succeed.

Academically, Emily was an achiever. She was determined to make it off the government assistance her family had lived on for most of her life.

But socially and emotionally, she was repeating the cycle. During her college years, Emily started drinking and "going home with someone different every night." Her sense of herself, that ugly feeling inside, was so all-consuming that she tried to alleviate it with the wrong kind of attention and acceptance, responding to any guy who noticed her, whether she was attracted to him or not. She didn't realize it at the time and excused her behavior to "just being a college kid." But looking back, Emily now understands the truth.

"It's textbook, what I went through," says Emily. "I slipped into a pattern."

Emily didn't like to be on her own for long. She kept seeking affirmation, replacing one man with another in order to feel desired. She had two children along the way with different men. The lower her self-esteem, the lower her standards became.

Many women and men alike may accept the first person who comes along and says, "Oh, you are all right," or who simply satisfies a biological need because they don't think they're going to get anyone better.

It wasn't until she began repeating the pattern of violence in her relationships that Emily made a real change. That was the line she could not cross. Emily was not going to allow her own children to be children of domestic violence.

UNDERSTANDING WHY WE FEEL SELF-CONSCIOUS

Today, Emily is fully aware of the connection between her relationship choices and her childhood. And awareness here is the key. Her whole perception of what a relationship is and her view of herself, her sense of her own attractiveness, has been distorted by what she experienced.

"Growing up with domestic violence robs us of our childhood and destroys our sense of what a healthy relationship should be like in the future," she says. "I've never had a healthy relationship, I repeated the cycle of violence in which I grew up. What I witnessed as a child destroyed my perceptions of what a healthy relationship should be.

"Looking back I was with those men because I didn't think I deserved anything more. Based on what I knew growing up, I didn't believe I could do any better than what I had."

Emily finally reached out for help and got involved with a support group that helps those in situations like hers. Meeting other people like her made Emily realize she wasn't alone and that she was strong and compassionate enough to help others whose circumstances were worse than hers. "Until then I never knew the meaning of real friendship; of total acceptance," says Emily. "It is so simple, so liberating, to be able to relate to other people."

Now she helps others get the same opportunity by working with nonprofits, getting involved in leadership training for the organizations, and writing on her blog, which has thousands of followers from all over the world. The women with whom she's in contact, both face-to-face and through social media, have shared their own stories and helped her unlearn the lies.

"For so many years I couldn't be happy with what I saw in the mirror. But now I know the truth that I have a heart of gold and would do anything to help other people, and that makes me feel beautiful, inside and out."

Emily finally learned the truth: that affirmation or approval from others or starving herself to become thin wasn't going to fix the hurt or relieve the sense of worthlessness and unimportance she felt inside. But when she discovered the truths that counter the lies, everything changed.

Emily's childhood experiences gave her a deep insight into the suffering of others and an ability to understand. Even as a little girl, she'd always instinctively understood the lies that were hurting her mother and felt gratitude for all that her mother tried to do despite her circumstances. Emily recognized her mother's attractiveness, worth, and importance, even when her mother didn't. Eventually Emily learned to embrace that truth in herself.

WE WEAR OUR PAIN ON THE OUTSIDE

Your face and body reflect how you feel about yourself. When you look in the mirror and see someone who believes he or she is worthless, sad, alone, or angry, that's what you'll be showing to others. It's the kind of thinking that makes you feel like you don't deserve any better. But that's the lie that has been encoded into the minds of the almost one billion people alive today who grew up living with domestic violence.

Overwhelmed parents in a violent mood may even hurl insults at their children—calling them ugly, repulsive, worthless, or bad. These harsh words and unfair put-downs are emotionally deadly, causing an impressionable child unbearable pain and leaving behind invisible scars carried into adulthood. Verbal violence wrecks a child's self-confidence. It humiliates them and leads them to believing that they're unattractive and undeserving of love.

After all, if Mom or Dad says so, it must be true. "Then I *am* ugly."

Conditioned to believe these lies, cute little kids feel flawed and imperfect, crying themselves to sleep, confused and discouraged. They ask themselves, "What's wrong with me?"

Even as adults, we berate ourselves, convinced we are unappealing, that our physicality is fatally flawed. We are simply *not enough*. And we certainly can't compare to the images we see in magazines and on TV.

Even if we could, it would make no difference. The degrading comments we have heard override reality. The insults actually hurt more than the physical blows. One woman who was a child of domestic violence recently told me: "You know, I could handle the beatings. But I couldn't stand being called fat or ugly one more time."

These words leave you feeling damaged and diminished. You don't believe in yourself. And your negative self-image affects everything. It becomes impossible for you to be objective about your looks.

As one thirteen-year-old girl recently confessed: "I'm so insecure about my physical appearance that all I want to do is wear big sweatshirts and pants so no one can see my body. I do fifty jumping jacks, thirty crunches, twenty-five leg lifts, and run every night. Do you think by doing this I'll lose weight? Please give me advice on what to do."

Feeling intense body shame, these young people often avoid

social interactions because they feel inadequate. By the time they're young adults, their distorted self-image has already wreaked havoc.

Cloé Madanes, a therapist and founder of Strategic Family Therapy, explains how low self-esteem can quickly create a self-fulfilling prophecy. Body language starts to reflect the insults that echo inside the mind: slouching bodies and downcast faces that give an air of depression, sadness, or shyness. Everything seems drained of energy.

WHEN NONPHYSICAL VIOLENCE CAUSES THE GREATEST PAIN

Suzanne grew up in a small housing development in the Midwest, where she witnessed a decade of violent arguments. When Suzanne was ten, her father divorced her mother. "My dad was miserable, and I can't blame him. My mother was constantly verbally abusive toward him. He was a real estate attorney, and a great guy. I'm not really sure what was wrong between them, but my mother made his life a living hell. So of course he left, and I was left with my mother."

Soon after the split, Suzanne's mother, Pat, began dating Guy, "who was basically a professional sponge," says Suzanne. "He started off as the most wonderful man in the world—so much fun, a great cook, very attentive—and he totally charmed his way into our lives. I wanted them to get married right away."

But after a few months, her mother was drinking heavily and acting verbally abusive with him. Then Guy began doing the same, and things escalated quickly.

Suzanne's mother would then take it out on her: "Anything he said to *her*, she'd say to *me*, like her stomach was too big and to 'suck it in, suck it in!'" To relieve herself from her own pain, she piled it onto her daughter, making her feel worthless. "Putting me down made her feel powerful and better about herself. But I just ended up hating myself."

In reality, Suzanne was an attractive, normal-weight young girl. She loved the outdoors and had a natural exuberance, but under the barrage of her mother's insults, she felt that she was unlovable and ugly. "I was by no means fat. In fact, my mother was so busy paying Guy's bills and buying cigarettes and alcohol with my dad's child support payments that she wasn't feeding me properly."

But because it was her mother saying these things, Suzanne took everything she said to heart and lost her self-confidence. "I *did* feel ugly," she says. "And I hated myself. I didn't feel like I was worth anything unless a guy liked me."

Seeing how her mother defined her self-worth by having a boyfriend, Suzanne quickly learned to do the same. By the time she was thirteen, she had a nineteen-year-old boyfriend.

"I was always attracted to powerhouses—boys who were controlling, who would tell me what to wear, what to do, how to fix my hair, and where I was going. I'd let them walk all over me."

As Suzanne hit her teenage years, she began having nightmares and panic attacks. She couldn't concentrate at school, and she began starving herself, desperate to become thinner. When the symptoms of anorexia became unmistakable, Suzanne's mom got her daughter into a treatment facility, where she admitted that: "I want to live in a tomb filled with gold. There will be no other people to look at me, especially no boys or men. I don't want to get married. I just want to be so rich that people leave me alone." She was ready to commit a kind of emotional suicide in order to escape the negative judgment of others.

And yet she was so physically attractive that, at twenty-one, she competed in a state beauty pageant, but even then, "I felt I had to wear a ton of stage makeup to try to cover up and improve myself," she says.

For children of domestic violence, feeling attractive has nothing to do with vanity. We didn't get the positive reinforcement that we deserved, the compliments and validation that every child needs. Because of our environment we were conditioned to feel defective, physically flawed, and inferior, and that profoundly altered the way we see ourselves. Even if we did not bear the brunt of insults, we either bore the brunt of silence or came to our own negative conclusions because we didn't have the developed brain to rationally come to any other conclusion.

As Professor Sandra Graham-Bermann reflected in our interview: "Children need to hear things like: 'Aren't you a cutie? You're so sweet. What a nice strong boy you are. Wow, you can really hit that ball well.' But when that doesn't happen, they conclude that they're just not valuable because they're so inept and unattractive."

TRANSFORMING THE LIE OF BEING SELF-CONSCIOUS

Transforming the lie of being self-conscious begins with awareness, with unlearning the lies. Only through awareness and understanding combined can children of domestic violence realize the truth—that feeling self-conscious is more based on how you feel about yourself than how you look physically.

Of course, you may want to make physical changes to your body. If we've lived these lies for a long time, our bodies may reflect that pain. Maybe we've spent years overeating, overdrinking, smoking, or watching way too much television in an attempt to bring some comfort to a life that had none in childhood.

Suzanne only recently started on a journey of self-acceptance. Her eating disorder was getting so out of hand that she was checked into a facility; nearly dying from the condition was the turning point. As soon as she moved out of the house and away from her mother's influence, she made a decision to eat better. She walks for forty-five minutes every day and eats healthy foods. She's learning to care much less about what she sees in the mirror and focuses instead on living her truths and unlearning the lies. She also found a boyfriend who respects her and doesn't treat her like an object. "I used to think that I had to be like a model or something. Now I don't even care. I look good like I am."

Most of us are not actors, models, or beauty pageant winners. And it's not appropriate to hold ourselves up to that standard of being in the top tenth of 1 percent on the beauty scale. What makes us attractive are the inner qualities that we project into the world; the confidence reflected in our body language draws people toward us.

When we know the truths, our bodies become the reflection. We can stand up straight, look people in the eye, and walk with confidence. When we know the truths, we know we don't require plastic surgery, designer clothes, or stage makeup for people to notice.

FEAR OF BEING REJECTED

As we've seen from the stories of Emily and Suzanne, poor body image is a huge part of the lie of self-consciousness that affects many women who grew up living with domestic violence, but men feel it too. In fact, many of the men I've talked to for this book, including Martin, Jeremy, and Roger (whom you will meet in the next chapter), have disliked certain physical attributes they have and have tried to change them, whether it was a self-perception of physical weakness or, in my case, weight. Growing up, I was always comparing myself to others and coming up short. I found proof that someone didn't like me in the smallest things—a glance or a momentary pause—and imagined that kids were constantly talking behind my back.

One weekend when I was around twelve, I was swimming at the local pool, horsing around with my friends, and a girl that I liked started making fun of my swimsuit. It was too small, and, seeing my waist spill out over the sides, she joked that "Brian has love handles!" .

I was mortified. Sure, I was a little chunky, but a crack like that should have slid right off. Instead, that comment stuck with me, and I replayed it over and over in my mind to the point where I felt like I had to fix myself. I became obsessed.

That was the year that I started making some real money, working at a jewelry store in Newark, buying and selling whatever came through the store, no questions asked. But instead of buying a stereo or a bike with the money, I took it to a cheap plastic surgeon, who performed liposuction on me. I was wide awake and vividly remember that skinny rod being stuck into my side and seeing the fat being sucked out through the hose. It was disgusting.

Looking back, I cannot believe that my self-esteem was so fragile and that the surgeon actually took my money and performed liposuction on a twelve-year-old boy. I was so ashamed; I tried to keep that secret my entire life. But now I just see it as a perfect example of the lengths that I would go to feel better about myself. If anything, that drastic step of liposuction made me feel worse about myself.

THE KEY TO BEING ATTRACTIVE

It was only as I began to unlearn my own lies that I became less self-conscious and began to notice how people responded to me as someone who is attractive. It is easy to generate a thought that creates a feeling of being self-conscious when you believe you are guilty, resentful, sad, alone, angry, hopeless, worthless, fearful, self-conscious, and unloved. It's also hard to lose weight and have the body you want, for example, because the lie of guilt kills willpower. Even when you are physically beautiful, it's not something you can see when you look in the mirror because years of emotional hurt have left you feeling worthless. So feeling attractive is all tied up with undoing the lies we've talked about in this book.

Now that you know the tight interrelationship between inner feelings and outward appearances, you can take inventory of all those strengths that helped you get through the emotional pain of your childhood. If you believe the truth, that you truly are confident, accomplished, passionate, grateful, guided, compassionate, trusting, free, and loved, then it is difficult to feel self-conscious. As you remind yourself of these truths each day, you will begin to feel more comfortable in your own skin. So cultivate these emotions on a daily basis.

FROM THE LIE TO THE TRUTH

The Lie

You are unattractive and flawed and everyone is judging you so. You are self-conscious and feel not good enough. You rely on affirmations from others and look to external fixes to make you feel attractive.

The Why

When you believe you are guilty, resentful, sad, alone, angry, hopeless, worthless, fearful, and unlovable, when that is your identity, it is not possible to feel physically good enough. Harsh criticisms and put-downs early in life left behind these lies that have been carried into adulthood. Nonphysical violence wrecks children's self-confidence. It humiliates them and leads them to believe that they're unattractive and undeserving of love and it carries into adulthood.

The Truth

I am attractive. When I act as though I am free, compassionate, grateful, guided, trusting, accomplished, confident, and lovable I am more attractive and I feel more attractive. I enjoy doing things each day that make me feel more healthy and vital. Whenever I doubt that I am free, compassionate, grateful, guided, trusting, accomplished, confident, and lovable, I act as though I am, even if it feels unnatural, and I am mindful of the positive feeling that doing so creates in me and in others.

To Try

1. Pick one of your new truths: that you no longer feel guilty but are free or that you are no longer resentful but compassionate, for example. Focus on it for the next three days.

2. Read the "Truth" section from the chapter that covers that truth right before you go to bed, and again in the morning. See and feel yourself acting as the truth describes.

3. At the end of the day, write down the occasions when you embodied this truth and relive those moments in your mind. It is also OK to momentarily acknowledge where perhaps you did not live up to the truth; that simple recognition helps you move closer to the truth and further away from the lie. But focus most on the positive, the times when you lived your new truth, even if those moments were few.

11

UNLOVED TO LOVING

When we love, we always strive to become better than we are.

—Paulo Coelho, *The Alchemist*

These emotions—feeling guilty, resentful, sad, alone, angry, hopeless, worthless, fearful, self-conscious—are aspects of the most fundamental lie of all: That you are unloved, unlovable, and unworthy of love. This is among our greatest fears and, some would argue, is our greatest fear. Those who grow up living with domestic violence grow up with basic doubts about whether they even deserve to be loved or to love. Many spend their lives avoiding that feeling altogether.

Roger ("Rock") Lockridge struggled with this for most of his life. He was unconsciously convinced that if he got too deep in his love for another human being, he would ultimately be abandoned or betrayed. Why? Because the people he loved most, his parents, committed the ultimate betrayal, choosing violence over the safety and well-being of their children. Love was a feeling that simply was not meant for him.

Born and raised near Muddy Creek Mountain, in West Virginia,

Roger's childhood home was isolated. There was only one way in or out of this homestead, which was densely forested, and the home where Roger, his parents, and three siblings lived was backed by steep cliffs, making it impossible for anyone to leave the place without Roger's father knowing about it.

His dad could never hold down a steady job, although he did try to provide for his family. He was not a bad man. Roger is quick to point out that, when sober, his dad was a loving guy who'd walk through a snowstorm to get diapers and milk for his kids. But he never committed to quit drinking and, when he drank, he became a monster. He didn't take it out directly on his kids, but he would get physically and verbally violent with Roger's mother, leaving Roger, the eldest boy, terrified for her safety.

Late one night, when Roger was ten, the fighting escalated to the point where Roger's mom thought it best to take herself and her children out of his way and wait out the drunken rage at her mother-in-law's house, a tiny cabin close by the family home. The plan backfired. The moment her kids were ushered inside their grandmother's house they turned around to see their father standing in the doorway with a rifle pointed at them, threatening to kill them all.

"Having a gun pointed at you is traumatic enough under any circumstance," says Roger, "but when it's your father on the trigger end of that gun . . ." To Roger, this seemed the ultimate proof that he was unlovable.

IF I BELIEVE I AM UNLOVED AND UNLOVABLE . . .

Like many children who grew up in violent families, Roger felt abandoned, deserted, and detached, and the impact on his sense of self was devastating. As Bruce Perry, founder of the Child Trauma Academy in Houston and professor of psychiatry at Northwestern University, explains:

> Being harmed by the people who are supposed to love you, being abandoned by them, being robbed of the one-on-one relationships that allow you to feel safe and valued, and to become humane—are profoundly destructive experiences. Because humans are inescapably social beings, the worst catastrophes that can befall us inevitably involve relationship loss. You cannot love yourself unless you have been loved and are loved.[1]

The need to be loved is a fundamental human need and a core part of our humanity. "Our sense of self depends on our relationships with others, and in many ways, we only know who we are by thinking about other people," explains Kelly McGonigal.[2] In other words, we are naturally social, and when we are children we cannot differentiate between self and others.

Recent studies and technological breakthroughs have allowed science to go even further in describing the precise dynamics of the connection between mother and infant and its impact on human psychology. Bruce Perry has studied the ways in which parental love or abuse can have powerful effects on a child's mental, physical, and emotional development. Among other things, he has found the devastating effects of separation anxiety.

Whenever a baby is separated from her mother, even briefly, she will go through a temporary protest phase, which accelerates the child's heart rate, raises the body temperature, creates a 600 percent spike in the stress hormone cortisol, and increases adrenaline levels. While reconnecting with the mother immediately corrects the problem, prolonged separation creates significant physical and emotional changes: growth hormone levels drop, cardiovascular functions decrease, sleep functions are disturbed, cognitive growth stops, and the immune system's strength plummets.

So, right from the start, love is a condition necessary for our ability to thrive, no less vital than milk. When we are born, we need to be touched. A newborn clings to her mother, and the powerful hormone oxytocin creates a profound bond between them. This "cuddle chemical" is essential for milk production, nursing, and the mother's ability to bond with her offspring. It triggers a feeling of profound connection. In this blissful state, a child basks in the comfort of a mother's arms knowing the world is a safe place to be.

But if when we are born we are routinely deprived of touch and affection, the consequences are severe, the possible result being the so-called failure to thrive syndrome.[3] This occurs when a baby is ignored, perfunctorily fed, or left alone. A child will despair and become unresponsive. In extreme cases, the baby may even stop eating, waste away, and die. That's how essential it is for humans to be shown that they are loved. In the same way that infants may fail to thrive when they do not experience the physical signs of love, when children grow up living with domestic violence, they learn to question how loved they are.

UNLEARNING THE LIE THAT WE ARE UNLOVABLE

The standoff between Roger's father and the family seemed to last forever. But after some time, the police came and Roger's dad ran off into the woods behind the house. The trooper put the family into his cruiser and drove them to a local shelter, which would become their home for the next four months.

It was the first time in his life that Roger felt there was help, that somebody cared. Each day he was at the shelter, Roger was exposed to people who dedicated their lives to helping families. It made a huge impression. "Yes, they are doing a job," he recalls, "but no one gets paid enough to do this—to commit to being there for people at the lowest point in their lives."

Roger was fortunate in that the people at the shelter acted as the One for him at a very young age. They helped him unlearn some of the most damaging lies about himself. At that moment he saw that he was not alone and he felt safe enough to trust. They had compassion for him, which let him know that he had been hurt. So therefore, he was then able to have compassion for himself and only then was he able to have compassion for others. He expressed his gratitude freely and promised himself that one day he would give back in the same way that they had given to him. He learned that it is never the job of a child to control the actions of an adult. He realized what had happened in his family was not his fault and that it was not his job to stop it. So his guilt began to subside, which set him free. As he unlearned the lies, he began to find evidence to support his new truths, and thus his transformation slowly began. Roger and his family were able to leave the refuge eventually and moved into a small apartment. Roger's mother reconnected with old friends, and made new ones while her kids settled into a more peaceful routine in their new schools. But with so many emotional issues unresolved, Roger's mother went a little too far enjoying her newfound freedom and started staying out late and drinking. She too became an alcoholic, often partying at home and attracting the attention of neighbors, who intervened when they felt her lifestyle might be harmful to the children.

But this time when somebody tried to help, there was an unintended consequence: Child Protective Services took Roger and his siblings away from their mother, who went into rehab. And, as it happened, their father was the only relative in the area who would take the kids.

Roger's father had convinced the authorities that he'd gotten clean, found a new job, and had his life back in order. It wasn't true. The family home had been destroyed by a storm, so the entire family had to move into their grandmother's tiny cabin, which had no indoor plumbing. Filthy, neglected, and isolated, they were forced to relive their old memories for the next four months.

It was here that Roger's new truths kicked in and he was able to use what he learned to convince a school counselor that he and his siblings needed help. By then, his mother had come out of rehab and found another job, and they were reunited.

This reunion was an important time for Roger as he found himself living his new truths, sharing that example with his family. He started to feel connected, he says, "in a way that I had never felt before."

It was also during this time that he overheard something that would stay with him for the rest of his life.

Unaware that he was within earshot, one of the police officers working his family's case told a social worker, "You know, what's really sad about this is that we just saved these kids, and ten years from now we are going to be arresting them."

Rather than getting angry at that comment, Roger chose to convert that feeling of rage into passion, and rather than believing what he heard and thinking all was hopeless, he now had a purpose. From that moment on, Roger vowed not only that he would prove the police officer wrong but that he would end up helping people like himself. He was thirteen years old.

BECOMING LESS SELF-CONSCIOUS

Fast-forward to high school: Roger and his family were moving on with their lives. But a lingering issue for Roger was his belief that he was unlovable, that no woman would ever want him. Even though he had unlearned many of the lies, this one stuck with him. He was the skinny little kid who always got picked on. He was shy and withdrawn and shut himself off from friendships. As for dating and relationships, he says, "I never believed I was meant to have a steady girlfriend, let alone a wife and children."

When one of his high school teachers couldn't remember his name, he'd earned the nickname "Rock," a shortened form of Roger Lockridge. Still a scrawny kid at the time, the moniker was used ironically, but Roger didn't care. He wanted to become "that guy his father never was—a rock—someone you could lean on." That's when he discovered weight training. Roger was sick of feeling weak and defenseless, so when he was a senior he decided he was going to get bigger and stronger. He saved up for some free weights and started working out at home. A few months later, he joined a local health club where he found the role models he was looking for.

As he envisioned a new self, he no longer felt worthless. Instead he felt accomplished. One accomplishment built on another. His fear of failure was replaced with a feeling of confidence. This confidence made him want to keep at it each week, and as he unlearned the lie of worthlessness, he became less self-conscious and was able to reveal his true self to the world.

As soon as he graduated high school, Roger took a job at a local shelter, the Family Refuge Center, handling files, getting coffee for the caseworkers, and answering the phones. He was keeping his promise to serve. It was a small role, but being that first voice someone heard on the end of the phone was a duty he took seriously. When government funds dried up and he lost his position, Roger found work wherever he could—anything from managing a health club to waiting tables—in order to fund his college education to get a degree in business.

During his final year in college, he got a call from his father, who told him he'd gone to rehab and was eager to make peace with his kids. Roger and his brother and sister went to see him in Salem, Virginia. Roger was now able to forgive his father, because of the compassion he had found in himself. It made this a far easier step to take than he imagined. Roger always knew deep down that his father loved him, but he could not connect those emotions with his father's actions. But now, Roger had come to understand what his father had been going through. The reconciliation was to be a fresh new start, but shortly afterward Roger's dad was diagnosed with terminal cancer, and he passed away a few months later.

Even though Roger felt that he was robbed of the love that his father could only now express, he knew what to do. He had learned (as Sonja Lyubomirsky articulated), "the next step after acknowledging regrets is to move on by committing ourselves to new pursuits."

SHARING THE TRUTHS WILL MAKE YOU FEEL LOVED

Roger found a career for himself in the bodybuilding field and it took off as he became nationally known for the columns he wrote for Bodybuilding.com. Meanwhile, he started volunteering back at the Family Refuge Center, getting more involved in mentoring children of domestic violence. During Domestic Violence Awareness Month he wrote an article about the story of his childhood and how bodybuilding helped him develop both his physical and emotional strength. He was amazed that many other men from the fitness world wrote in to say they grew up living with domestic violence. Suddenly Roger had a way to connect and help millions around the world.

The accolades for his article got him local news coverage and the attention of West Virginia's governor—a platform that Roger has since leveraged to become an outspoken advocate for people who grew up living with domestic violence. The two careers have dovetailed perfectly. Bodybuilding.com recently launched a social media awareness campaign, using Roger as the poster boy with the slogan, "As a fitness writer, I work to help my generation; as a child advocate, I work to help the next generation."

Roger now sits on the board of the Family Refuge Center and serves as their media spokesman as well as a part-time caseworker, helping children record their stories so they don't have to relive it several times, like he did. He's the first person in the history of the center to go from resident to caseworker to board member, and he's fiercely proud of his connection.

WHEN YOU SHARE THE TRUTHS WITH OTHERS, LOVE APPEARS

In writing and researching this book, a common theme emerges with respect to the emotion of love and how growing up with domestic violence warps it. Take Roger, for example. Considering what he has come through and the man he has become, he is as deserving of love as anyone. But for a long time, he didn't see it that way. He still felt, deep down, that he was unlovable and unworthy. To be more precise, the only way he felt he deserved to feel loved would be if he earned it.

As Roger's experience showed him, only after consistently sharing the truths with others was he able to attract the type of love that comes from being deeply intimately connected to another person. "It took a long time for me to accept that I was deserving of it because I didn't feel I earned it."

By sharing the truths, he eventually attracted another who never had to unlearn the lies. It took Roger time to understand and accept the simple fact that someone could love him unconditionally and that he could give that love back without fear. "My life changed," he says, "when I fully accepted the truth that I could be loved."

So the lesson here is clear. As you unlearn the lies and share the truths with others, you can help them feel free, compassionate, grateful, hopeful, trusting, passionate, accomplished, confident, and attractive. You never need to worry about earning love because it will come to you. And when it does, you can happily accept it and give more love in return.

Roger has become a role model to countless people who grew up living with domestic violence. He is a loving husband and father to two boys. He has fully embraced the truth of love. Growing up, he desperately wanted to find that strong man, that rock in his own life, and he never did, so instead, he says, "I became the man I wanted to be and the father I wanted to have because I want to speak to future generations before they repeat the pattern and help them reach their full potential."

I DIDN'T UNDERSTAND WHAT LOVE MEANT

Growing up, we never used the word *love*. We didn't show physical affection. But there was no doubt that I felt a deep, tender caring for my mother's well-being. And as I look back I know there was love around me, I just couldn't see it through all the fear and confusion. There were moments that I remember. When I was a toddler, my mother would tuck me in after returning from work. She'd put my *Bad News Bears* teddy bear right next to me and lie down beside me in the bed. I remember how her crisp waitress uniform would crackle as she lay down and how much I loved the smell of restaurant food mixed with her perfume and the spray starch she ironed into her blouse. I have always loved that smell because it meant everything was safe.

She would sometimes read to me, often from *Goodnight Moon*—the classic children's book by Margaret Wise Brown. I felt such comfort looking at those images of the red balloon and the cow jumping over the moon, the bears, and the kittens and the mittens and the quiet old lady whispering, "hush." I felt so happy to have her in the room, instead of with Keith, because it made me feel certain that, for that brief moment, nothing could happen.

But something always broke the spell of those peaceful storybook nights that the book promised. For every moment of peace, security, and kindness, there were just as many moments of fear and pain. Much later in the night, I would hear the loud voices, and I remember repeating the phrase "goodnight noises" to myself as I sat atop the stairs in the hope of somehow ending the fighting.

As I got older, there was no more tucking in. The fights grew more intense, my mother grew more depressed, and my sister ran away. Those moments of tenderness just made me feel more exposed and vulnerable—more wounded when their promise came crashing down—so I gave up on them forever. To deaden the pain, I instinctively grew numb to any form of love.

ACCOMPLISHED AT EVERYTHING—EXCEPT LOVING AND BEING LOVED

The impact of feeling unloved can carry forward for decades. On the surface, Amanda, a lawyer at a top Manhattan firm, has everything. But her extraordinary accomplishments and busy lifestyle leave her feeling empty inside.

She was born to an unhappy, violent couple and grew up as an only child in the shadow of their quarrels. They were so preoccupied with their fights and the emotional fallout, as Amanda remembers it, that they basically stopped attending to her. Her mother would stay in her room all day, the blinds drawn. Her father would disappear all weekend. By age seven she was expected to pick out her own clothes, get dressed, make her own breakfast, and get to school on time, while her mother stayed in bed. Her mother never asked her about friends at school, where she went in the afternoons, or when she'd be back. At home she would watch television alone for hours at a time.

As we've discovered through the other stories in this book, all too often children who have lived with domestic violence have been raised by adults who themselves were children of domestic violence. Their parents were not role models of loving behavior. And we know how important it is during this time that the parents' responses are rational and not emotional. But children don't have that kind of perspective. They simply take the weight of the blame on their own shoulders. They feel emotionally abandoned, convinced that they're both *unloved* and *unlovable*.

While the feeling of being unloved may be true at this moment, being unlovable is a lie. This is a damaging falsehood that makes children of domestic violence believe that they are unworthy of tenderness or care.

Of course, all children are lovable and deserve to feel that way. When they don't, it's confusing and terrifying to admit: *My parents don't love me.* This psychic pain is the worst kind of punishment—just as destructive as physical abuse. In fact, children who feel unloved suffer as much or more psychologically as if they had been physically abused.

Although Amanda proved to be an especially adaptable child on the surface, both at home and at school, she suffered from her parents' emotional neglect, a nonphysical violence.

"Sometimes I tried to be extra nice to my parents, making them breakfast in the morning, somehow hoping that I could influence them enough to stop fighting with each other, but it never worked. In the end, that kind of isolation changes who you become. You start to feel like you can survive without feelings or love or anything."

By the time Amanda reached high school, she had become an obsessive overachiever. She graduated near the top of her class and earned a scholarship to an excellent university. She then went on to law school and now works as a partner at a prestigious law firm. "I just decided that I was going to work harder than anyone else," she remembers. "It was almost a feeling of revenge. Like I'm going to make everyone regret writing me off."

Her attitude worked at one level, shaping the early success of her legal career—but it nearly ruined her marriage. Her husband, a college sweetheart who earned a decent living as a corporate accountant, couldn't understand why his wife needed to put in such long hours and resented her twelve-hour workdays. It was at work where she got all of her love and connection, where she felt worthy, so that is where she put her time. While Amanda had avoided repeating the cycle of her parents' violent relationships, she had problems stemming from chronic workaholism and challenges with personal intimacy. Yet, she recalls the birth of her daughter as a revealing moment: "When I saw her little fingers reach up to me, and when I held her in my arms, I think that was the first time I ever felt a surge of anything like love go through me. I'd never experienced anything like it before. It was confusing. I had tears in my eyes, but at the same time, I felt this panic, because I realized that I had no idea how to be a good mother. My own ability to love was sabotaged by my childhood. I had absolutely no idea what love meant."

Despite this epiphany, Amanda did not resolve the emotional distance she kept between herself and the world, and her marriage continued to deteriorate. She worked obsessively, became verbally abusive, and grew increasingly estranged from her husband. It took the threat of a divorce, and the prospect of becoming a single mother, for Amanda to finally acknowledge the harm that she was doing to herself and her family. "My family was crumbling and it was my fault. My daughter was having behavioral problems in school, my husband had moved out, and I was refusing to acknowledge how much I was actually hurting inside. I had set up this entire bubble to keep all my feelings out of my life. It was unsustainable."

MASKING THE PAIN OF FEELING UNLOVED

When we feel unloved, we tend to unconsciously sabotage our own relationships or overcompensate for the pain by excelling in other areas. We carry around a core belief that others will dislike us. We cannot imagine that we're worthy of love, so we find ways to either keep others at bay or dazzle them with our talent.

Amanda had a hard time facing up to her own feelings, even when she committed herself to saving the marriage by scaling back her law practice. Her turning point came one day during her morning commute.

"I was riding the bus, just like any other day, when I struck up a conversation with the person sitting next to me, which I never do. It turns out that she was a professor of comparative religion and she had studied most major religions since their inception to determine the shared essential message of each. Jokingly, I asked her if she could tell me the secret to life because I could sure use some advice. 'That's simple,' she said. 'Do unto others as you would have them do unto you. It all comes down to that.'

"I must say that I really didn't think much of her answer at the time. I had a hard time taking her seriously. It was too simple. Too unsophisticated. Too obvious. But something about her confidence when she said it stuck with me. I mean she studied this for her entire life."

Amanda began to pay more attention to how she treated others, and the impact it had on her own feelings. With the same drive that characterized her approach to everything else in her life, she dedicated herself to making others feel the feelings that she most wanted inside herself.

"I gave it a try. I ended up volunteering at a couple places. I started offering compliments to the people around me, to colleagues at work. I began showing affection and appreciation for my husband and giving more love and attention to our young daughter, whose face lit up every time I opened my arms to give her a hug. As awkward as I felt at first, people started treating me noticeably better. They made me feel better about myself."

Amanda's story offers a simple but powerful message. Those of us who grew up living with domestic violence missed learning some important lessons about love—some of the fundamental building blocks about how loving people treat each other. Most important, we missed out on discovering that we are worthy of love! We never really had the chance to discover our value through someone else's eyes.

Tony Robbins puts it best when he describes the difference he notices in those who have been exposed to childhood domestic violence. "Someone who's gone through it develops spiritual strength," Robbins told me. While these experiences don't automatically make that person more compassionate, they have the potential. "It doesn't have to be pain that lasts the rest of your life," Robbins continues. "It's not that you won't feel the pain, but that experience can give you more compassion for other people and it can motivate you to serve another, helping someone else make it through."

Both Roger and Amanda had made great strides in their lives. They've overcome many of the lies they were living with—guilt, anger, and worthlessness—and built fulfilling lives for themselves. Roger came to embody his nickname Rock, a pillar of strength and the father he'd been missing in his own life. Amanda dealt with the neglect and lack of love in her early years by becoming highly self-sufficient, taking care of herself and others as an over-achiever in all aspects of her life. The last piece that was missing was love: Amanda struggled to give; Roger found it hard to receive.

THE ULTIMATE TRUTH OF LOVE

Giving and receiving love is at the heart of reaching our full potential. As people who grew up living with domestic violence, we know what it's like to feel unloved, and we can understand the damage it can do to a developing mind. The lack of love is precisely why we have the hunger to reclaim that missing connection. And this need is the secret weapon embedded in this lie: We can turn the hollowness of feeling unloved into the strength of showing others the love we never felt as children.

Today, we have to make a fundamental choice between these two statements: I experienced an injustice when I was young and because of that the rest of the world should suffer, or I experienced an injustice when I was young and because of it nobody should ever have to go through that alone again.

How do we begin to make up for all the love we lacked as children? By sharing the truths we now know. By making others feel the way we want to feel deep inside. Making others feel free, compassionate, grateful, trusting, passionate, guided, accomplished, confident, attractive, and loved. By practicing empathy, and putting ourselves in the shoes of others. By building our sense of compassion, understanding the feelings of others, and trying to ease the suffering of others. Applaud someone's efforts instead of being judgmental. Be courteous instead of impatient. Replace criticism with heartfelt compliments. The response you get, in turn, will help reinforce the sense that you are loved. We receive love by giving it away, and we create love by taking action that supports it. Anytime you give love you create in you the ability to be loved in return.

GOODNIGHT MOON: MY MOTHER'S
LEGACY OF LOVE

Recently, my mother was diagnosed with cancer, and she has been battling it bravely. Her strength and optimism are sources of inspiration to me. I have seen that living with cancer has made her appreciate every moment of every day in a way that she never had before.

I think that if my mother hadn't become sick, she may have been less supportive of my writing this book. By helping us resolve the past and deepen our connection to one another, the cancer has been its own sort of blessing. At least, that is the meaning we're choosing to give it.

Looking back now, with all the perspective that time and experience has given me, I can without question say that my mother did the best she could with what she knew. She was overwhelmed, overworked, physically exhausted, stressed by financial pressure, and strung out by violence. She joined me recently for the birthday party of my seven-year-old daughter. The sight of them together in my backyard, smiling, was an image of love and family that I could never have imagined when I was young. Later that afternoon, I reminded her of one of my early birthdays and took the risk of asking her about Keith and whether she kept in touch with him. I tried to be nonchalant, but I'm sure that I didn't quite succeed.

"No, I don't," she replied curtly, as if to end the conversation. But then she looked up, and sensing something inside me, she paused to add, "You know, Brian, he went through some of the same things you did when he was young."

To hear her say those words, after everything that she had gone through, made me feel so proud. It wasn't just the compassion in her voice. It was her desire to help *me* understand, to reach beyond the anger and resentment coiled inside my question, and past her own guilt over the silence and sadness of those years we shared. She wanted to impart that small bit of wisdom to me, perhaps hoping it could erase some of the pain, but mostly, I believe, because I was her son and she loved me.

Later that month I had planned a trip for us. I do business in Europe, and it always saddened me to think that she had never seen that part of the world with her own eyes, so I invited her and her sister to join me to celebrate Mother's Day in Paris.

One evening a few days into our trip, about an hour before we were all to meet for dinner near our hotel, I was strolling through a bookshop and stumbled upon a familiar image—the cover of the children's book *Goodnight Moon*, translated into French as *Bonsoir Lune*.

As I thumbed through the book, I felt tears in my eyes, reflecting on how far my mother and I had come since those early days when she read it to me at night and how precious that memory remains to me even today. I picked up the book, found a nearby pen, and wrote a note to my mother on the inside cover of the book.

When I gave the book to her that evening after dinner, she smiled at the cover, her eyes welling with tears, and opened the book to read the inscription, "Dear Mom, for all the nights that you were there to read this to me. With all my love."

She began to cry and quietly put the book down and got up from the table. I thought she would return after she collected herself, but ten minutes later, I realized that she was not coming back.

Only later did I come to understand what she felt. Reading that book had given her as much comfort as it had given me. It made her feel like a good mother, yes—but being in my room was also a peaceful place *for her.* She knew that so long as she was tucking me in, nothing bad would happen.

That book, in a way, was the bedtime story that no one had ever read to her as a child. It was her own moment of peace. Back then, I think that it may have been the only peace she ever knew. To see that book, I believe, brought all those memories rushing back to her, and she felt overwhelmed by both love and sadness all at once.

As my mother faced the end of her life she found great comfort in knowing that we had both found safety and peace. The bond we shared in those brief moments, reading that book together, has grown and filled our entire lives with love. We have both come through the worst of it.

———————

This is my wish for everyone who grew up with domestic violence. All those lies—that you are guilty, resentful, sad, alone, angry, hopeless, worthless, fearful, self-conscious, and unloved—that you can see the truth. It can be done, because we are resilient, much stronger than we ever knew. When we discover that hidden strength, the truth is never far away.

As for my mother, the story ends happily. The doctors say that it was a miracle that the cancer subsided because, as they had told me very early on, she had less than a 5 percent chance to live.

You see, I knew she would live. With what she has overcome, with what she has inside of her, she is invincible. Of course she would overcome this obstacle.

She is now cancer free and rebuilding the most important relationships in her life. In many ways, at sixty-five, she has just unlearned what she learned for all of those years. She is now beginning to fully live and is reaching her true potential, proving yet again that it is never too late.

FROM THE LIE TO THE TRUTH

The Lie

You are unlovable and unworthy of love. You don't even really understand at times what love means. You are even uncomfortable using the word *love*, and you have a difficult time expressing it yourself. And this is the way it will always be. It's just who you are because you doubt whether you even deserve to be loved.

The Why

A lack of love early in life interferes with your sense of self. Fundamentally, we are social beings who define ourselves by our relations with others, beginning with that vital connection between parent and child. You believe you weren't loved by those who created you, so you wonder who else could ever truly love you.

The Truth

I am loved. I am loving.

I find opportunities to make others feel free, compassionate, grateful, trusting, passionate, guided, accomplished, confident, attractive, and loved. I give freely the feelings I most want to feel.

In doing so, I feel the same feelings. I feel loving and I feel loved.

I give these feelings freely as the love I give without expectation is love that comes back to me. By giving others the feelings that they most cherish in life, the same feelings are created in me.

To Try

1. Share with others the truths that you have learned, the truths that counter the lies. In your day-to-day conversations, do all that you can to make others feel free, compassionate, grateful, trusting, passionate, guided, accomplished, confident, attractive, and loved.

2. Give to yourself the acknowledgment and love that you share with others—allow yourself to feel it. The more you do so the more you will embody these truths, and the more they will become yours.

MY WISH FOR YOU

*A life is not important except in the impact it has on
other lives.*   —Jackie Robinson

We all have a picture of what we want our life to be about and
what we want to leave behind when we are no longer here. Every
day you are having an effect on the lives of others. If there's a
reason you went through what you did, then it has to be so others
won't have to. In the end, your life will be an example of what is
possible.

This is the ultimate truth. But the question is, Do you believe
it? Now that you've reached the end of this book, have you discovered and embraced your *invincibility*? Your inability to be conquered, to be overcome.

John Schindler, a renowned physician and leading expert on
the mind-body connection, believes that self-esteem is a fundamental need for every human being. It's not something that we
simply want or that would be nice to have, it's a *need*. We need to
feel esteem for self. I know this to be true not only because of the

data but because I see it in myself and in the lives of countless others.

So how do you meet this need? Simply by doing what you just did: something difficult. Whether you read the entire book or read the parts that brought you here, you did something difficult. You faced the lies that have been holding you back, and you made yourself aware of the truths. You cannot help but begin to make progress toward what you now know to be true. When the sun is up, you can't help but see more clearly.

The first step is always the most challenging, which is why too few ever take it. But you already have. While you now own these truths, understand that at times the lies will come back again. They will return as thoughts, those thoughts will trigger feelings, and those feelings will trigger actions.

You can choose to act in a way that moves you away from your full potential. Those thoughts and feelings may cause you to act in a way that hurts another or sabotages the progress that you have made. Or you can choose to act in a way that reinforces what you know to be true, and therein lies the secret.

You are in control of the meaning of your life. When you make the simple choice *not* to act in a way that derails you from realizing your dreams, it is a signal to your brain that the old pattern is no longer acceptable. As Norman Doidge explains, each time we try, we begin fixing bad connections and creating new ones. Even just from the effort. We effectively create new pathways in our brain, and we lay the groundwork for change. We may not be able to eliminate the feeling altogether, but we can choose not to act on it, and by making that choice, we unlearn what was learned. Do not get discouraged. There is nothing you can't handle; nothing through which you can't persevere.

You experienced an injustice in childhood that you wouldn't

wish on anyone. That is done. But during that time you were cultivating skills and traits in common with some of the most successful people who have ever lived. In fact, the biggest lie of all is this: *Because of what I experienced I can't.* But all this time you've had the strengths, those secret weapons that will transform the biggest lie into the biggest truth: *Because of what I experienced, I uniquely can.*

So you may say to yourself, "I know deep down that this is who I am, who I was meant to be. Maybe I haven't always lived these truths, but now I know this is who I am. So how can I make certain that I live the truths each day and guard against the lies?"

Like you, I don't want to leave something this important to chance. I want to do everything I can to feel and act each day in a way that is consistent with my true self. The good news is that there are two very simple things to do that will assure you get what you want.

First, each week choose a truth. You can start with the first chapter and move to the next, or you can pick and choose at will. It doesn't matter. Perhaps this week you have something coming up where you know your confidence needs to come through. Pick that truth and say it to yourself each morning while you are getting ready for your day and again right before you go to sleep. Keep it on your phone, or a piece of paper, or keep this book with you—whatever works. The more you repeat the truth to yourself, the more you will cultivate it, and the more it becomes a part of you. If you do nothing else each day, make certain to do this one thing.

Second, share what you have learned. Nothing is more powerful. Sharing is the pathway to the part of the brain that houses long-term storage. Share it with someone in need, with a close friend, a family member; the key is to share it. If you need any other suggestions, please visit us at cdv.org and reach out to us.

ACKNOWLEDGMENTS

I would like to acknowledge with a deep appreciation and gratitude:

All those who spend their career working to help better understand what happens to a person who grows up living with domestic violence.

Samantha Marshall, my collaborative writer, whose talent was essential in bringing the story of *Invincible* to life.

All those who selflessly and courageously told their stories so that we may find within them a piece of ourselves or of someone we care about.

My mom, Marilyn—you have taught me more than you will ever know. I love you.

My children, Ella and Frank, who fill me up with the truths and love each day and remind me of what is possible when you grow up living without domestic violence.

Anthony Robbins—for his generous heart and caring spirit, I am forever grateful.

Renee McDonald for her expertise, vision, and willingness to continually contribute.

Jeffrey Edelson for helping me and so many others obtain true awareness and understanding.

Sandra Graham-Bermann for her research, wisdom, and insight.

Todd Shuster for sharing this vision when few did.

Jacob Moore for his tireless work throughout the entire process.

Mark Brown and Glenn Plaskin for their magnificent insights at the beginning of this project.

My publisher and editor, John Duff, and all the other wonderful people at Perigee who made this book possible.

NOTES

Chapter 1: Undiscovered Gifts

1 UNICEF Child Protection Center and the Body Shop International, "Behind Closed Doors: The Impact of Domestic Violence on Children," 2006, unicef .org/protection/files/BehindClosedDoors.pdf.

2 Alison Gopnik, *The Philosophical Baby: What Children's Minds Tell Us About Truth, Love, and the Meaning of Life* (New York: Picador, 2010).

3 Kelly McGonigal, *The Willpower Instinct: How Self-Control Works, Why It Matters, and What You Can Do to Get More of It* (New York: Avery, 2011).

4 Bruce Perry and Maia Szalavitz, *The Boy Who Was Raised As a Dog and Other Stories from a Child Psychiatrist's Notebook: What Traumatized Children Can Teach Us About Loss, Love, and Healing* (New York: Basic Books, 2006).

5 UNICEF Child Protection Center and the Body Shop International, "Behind Closed Doors."

6 L. Silvern, J. Karyl, L. Waelde, et al., "Retrospective Reports of Parental Partner Abuse: Relationships to Depression, Trauma Symptoms and Self-Esteem Among College Students," *Journal of Family Violence* 10 (1995): 177–202.

7 National Scientific Council on the Developing Child, "Excessive Stress Disrupts the Architecture of the Developing Brain," Working Paper #3, Cambridge: Harvard University, 2005.

8 J. Avery, "Interparental Violence, Post Traumatic Stress, and Child Cognitive Functioning," MS Thesis, Wayne State University, Ann Arbor, Michigan, 2009.

9 Defending Children, "Report of the Attorney General's National Task Force on Children Exposed to Violence," 2012, justice.gov/defendingchildhood /cev-rpt-full.pdf.

10 Norman Doidge, *The Brain That Changes Itself: Stories of Personal Triumph from the Frontiers of Brain Science* (New York: Viking/Penguin Books, 2007).

11 E. F. Rothman, D. G. Mandel, and J. G. Silverman, "Abusers' Perceptions of the Effect of Their Intimate Partner Violence on Children," *Violence Against Women* 11 (2007): 1179–1191.

12 D. A. Wolfe, C. Wekerle, D. Reitzel, and R. Gough, "Strategies to Address Violence in the Lives of High Risk Youth," in *Ending the Cycle of Violence: Community Responses to Children of Battered Women*, eds. E. Peled, P. G. Jaffe, and J. L. Edleson (New York: Sage Publications, 1995).

13 Gopnik, *The Philosophical Baby*.

14 Stephen Joseph, *What Doesn't Kill Us: The New Psychology of Posttraumatic Growth* (New York: Basic Books, 2011).

15 "Tony Robbins' Tough Childhood," *Oprah's Next Chapter*, Oprah Winfrey Network, February 19, 2012, youtube.com/watch?v=gYxM0xOwK_Q.

16 Perry and Szalavitz, *The Boy Who Was Raised As a Dog*.

17 Joseph, *What Doesn't Kill Us*.

18 Perry and Szalavitz, *The Boy Who Was Raised As a Dog*.

19 Doidge, *The Brain That Changes Itself*.

20 McGonigal, *The Willpower Instinct*.

21 Kristin Neff, *Self-Compassion: Stop Beating Yourself Up and Leave Insecurity Behind* (New York: William Morrow, 2011).

22 Doidge, *The Brain That Changes Itself*.

Chapter 2: Guilty to Free

1 Rick Warren, *The Purpose Driven Life: What on Earth Am I Here For?* (Grand Rapids, MI: Zondervan, 2002).

2 John Bradshaw, *Healing the Shame That Binds You*, rev. ed. (Deerfield Beach, FL: Health Communications, Inc., 1988).

3 Richard J. McNally, *Remembering Trauma* (New York: Harvard University Press, 2005).

4 Sonja Lyubomirsky, *The Myths of Happiness: What Should Make You Happy, but Doesn't; What Shouldn't Make You Happy, but Does* (New York: Penguin Press, 2013).

5 Ibid.

6 William B. Stiles, Paul L. Shuster, and Jinni A. Harrigan, "Disclosure and Anxiety: A Test of the Fever Model," *Journal of Personality and Social Psychology* 63, no. 6 (1992): 980–988.

7 Joseph, *What Doesn't Kill Us*.

8 McGonigal, *The Willpower Instinct*.

Chapter 3: Resentful to Compassionate

1 Perry and Szalavitz, *The Boy Who Was Raised As a Dog.*
2 Warren, *The Purpose Driven Life.*
3 Sarah Blaffer Hrdy, *Mother Nature: Maternal Instincts and How They Shape the Human Species* (New York: Ballantine Books, 2000).
4 Lyubomirsky, *The Myths of Happiness.*
5 Warren, *The Purpose Driven Life.*
6 Ibid.
7 R. Douglas Fields, *The Other Brain: The Scientific and Medical Breakthroughs That Will Heal Our Brains and Revolutionize Our Health* (New York: Simon & Schuster, 2011).
8 Louann Brizendine, *The Male Brain* (New York: Harmony, 2011).
9 Carsten Wrosch, "Can Blaming Others Make People Sick?" *Concordia University News,* Montreal, August 9, 2011, http://www.concordia.ca/cunews/main/releases/2011/08/09/can-blaming-others-make-people-sick.html.
10 John McTernan, "Nelson Mandela Had a Unique Gift: He Was Able to Govern in Poetry," *Telegraph,* December 6, 2013, blogs.telegraph.co.uk/news/johnmc ternan1/100248969/nelson-mandela-had-a-unique-gift-he-was-able-to-govern-in-poetry.
11 Michelle Johnson, "Depression Caused by Domestic Abuse," Examiner .com, April 24, 2010, examiner.com/domestic-violence-abuse-in-national/depression-caused-by-domestic-abuse.
12 Bill Clinton, *My Life* (New York: Vintage, 2005).
13 Kathryn Spink, *Mother Teresa* (New York: HarperCollins, 1998).
14 Mohandas K. Gandhi, *All Men Are Brothers* (Delhi, India: Rajpal and Sons, 2012).

Chapter 4: Sad to Grateful

1 Boyle, P. Jones, and S. Lloyd, "The Association between Domestic Violence and Self Harm in Emergency Medicine Patients," *Emergency Medicine Journal* 23, no. 8 (2006): 604–607, ncbi.nlm.nih.gov/pmc/articles/PMC2564159.
2 Janell Matula, "Self-Injury/Cutting," *Stand Up Against Domestic Violence,* June 9, 2011, standupagainstdomesticviolence.webs.com/apps/blog/show/7334386-self-injury-cutting.
3 S. M. Sergeant and M. Mongrain, "Promoting Gratitude: Advantages for Those Vulnerable to Depression," paper presented at the 117th American Psychological Association Symposium, Toronto, Canada, 2009.

4   P. C. Watkins, K. Woodward, T. Stone, and R. L. Kolts, "Gratitude and Happiness: Development of a Measure of Gratitude, and Relationships with Subjective Well-Being," *Social Behavior and Personality* 31, no. 5 (2003): 431–452.
5   Lyubomirsky, *The Myths of Happiness.*

Chapter 5: Alone to Trusting

1   K. Henning, H. Leitenberg, P. Coffey, et al., "Long-Term Psychological and Social Impact of Witnessing Physical Contact between Parents," *Journal of Interpersonal Violence* 11, no. 1 (1996): 35–51.
2   Perry and Szalavitz, *The Boy Who Was Raised As a Dog.*
3   Ann Shields and Dante Cicchetti, "Reactive Aggression among Maltreated Children: The Contributions of Attention and Emotion Dysregulation," *Journal of Consulting and Clinical Psychology* 27 (1998): 381–395.
4   Daniel Schechter, "Caregiver Traumatization Adversely Impacts Young Children's Mental Representations on the MacArthur Story-Stem Battery," *Attachment and Human Development* 9, no. 3 (2007): 187–205.
5   Lyubomirsky, *The Myths of Happiness.*
6   Gopnik, *The Philosophical Baby.*

Chapter 6: Angry to Passionate

1   Gopnik, *The Philosophical Baby.*
2   R. Douglas Fields, "Why Girls Are More Vulnerable to Maltreatment," Brainfacts.com, November 2013, blog.brainfacts.org/2013/11/why-girls-are-more-vulnerable-to-maltreatment/#.Ux8u89fD_IU.
3   Joseph, *What Doesn't Kill Us.*
4   Brizendine, *The Male Brain.*
5   Fields, *The Other Brain.*
6   Albert E. N. Gray, "The Common Denominator of Success," http://lifestyle sales.files.wordpress.com/2012/02/thecommondenominatorofsuccess-albertengray.pdf.
7   A. C. Baldry, "Bullying in Schools and Exposure to Domestic Violence," *Child Abuse and Neglect* 27, no. 7 (July 2003): 713–732.

Chapter 7: Hopeless to Guided

1   Viktor E. Frankl, *Man's Search for Meaning* (New York: Beacon Press, 2006).
2   Howard Gardner, "Howard Gardner's Theory of Multiple Intelligences," Genius, cse.emory.edu/sciencenet/mismeasure/genius/research02.html.

3 Joseph, *What Doesn't Kill Us.*
4 Daniel Kahneman, *Thinking, Fast and Slow* (New York: Farrar, Straus and Giroux, 2013).

Chapter 8: Worthless to Accomplished

1 Warren, *The Purpose Driven Life.*
2 Joseph, *What Doesn't Kill Us.*

Chapter 9: Fearful to Confident

1 Lyubomirsky, *The Myths of Happiness.*
2 Perry and Szalavitz, *The Boy Who Was Raised As a Dog.*
3 Brené Brown, "Want to Be Happy? Stop Trying to Be Perfect," CNN Living, November 1, 2010, cnn.com/2010/LIVING/11/01/give.up.perfection.
4 Warren, *The Purpose Driven Life.*
5 Lyubomirsky, *The Myths of Happiness.*

Chapter 10: Self-Conscious to Attractive

1 Brizendine, *The Male Brain.*

Chapter 11: Unloved to Loving

1 Perry and Szalavitz, *The Boy Who Was Raised As a Dog.*
2 McGonigal, *The Willpower Instinct.*
3 "Failure to Thrive," Clinical Key, Elsevier, clinicalkey.com/topics/pediatrics /failure-to-thrive.html.

INDEX

accomplished. *See* worthless to accomplished
acknowledging regrets and commitment to new pursuits, unloved to loving, 228
action, taking
  DATA (Decide, Ask, Truth, Act), 103, 140–41, 142–43
  fearful to confident, 188–89
  guilty to free, 28, 29, 36–37, 38, 43–45, 45–46, 47, 50–53, 54
Adam's story, 134–36, 138, 139
addiction, guilt as, 38
adrenaline, 96, 223
adversity and happiness, 101
Aguilera, Christina, 13
Alabama, 125
Alchemist, The (Coelho), 221
alcohol abuse. *See* substance abuse
alone to trusting, 23, 24, 105–24
  assuming positive intent, 121, 123
  brain and, 105, 112–13, 118–19
  cycle of domestic violence, 115–16
  Eleanor's story, 105, 107–12, 118
  emotional thinking, 118–19
  From the Lie to the Truth, 122–24
  gateway to trust, 120–21
  intimacy, 106, 112, 121
  Julia's story, 114–18
  keeping others at a distance, 111–13, 122
  keys to trust, 121–22
  knowing yourself and trusting, 114–20, 122, 123, 124
  life narrative, 121

One, the (helping to unlearn what was learned), 110, 111
  other lies, 204, 217, 221, 240–42
  physical violence, 107, 115
  rational thinking, 119
  relationships and, 105–6, 108, 109, 111, 112, 122
  risk taking, 106, 117, 118, 121, 123–24
  sharing as key to freedom, 106, 110, 230
  society's basic moral value (trust), 121
  suspicions of others, 118–19
  trust and knowing yourself, 114–20, 122, 123, 124
  verbal violence, 115
  See also children of domestic violence
Amanda's story, 232, 233–34, 235–36
amygdala, 68, 129, 130, 184
angry to passionate, 23, 24, 125–43
  Adam's story, 134–36, 138, 139
  blame, taking away your power, 127–29
  brain and, 126, 129–30, 133
  changing the pattern, 134–36
  control from anger, 129–31, 136–67
  controlling your anger, 137–38, 142
  cost of anger, 136–37
  cycle of domestic violence, 126
  DATA (Decide, Ask, Truth, Act), 103, 140–41, 142–43
  fight-or-flight reaction, 129, 131
  From the Lie to the Truth, 141–43

insignificance and anger, 125, 129
Jeremy's story, 125–29, 131–34, 139
men vs. women, 130
other lies, 204, 217, 221,
    240–42
physical violence, 125, 126, 135, 136
questioning the anger, 134–36
redirecting anger's energy toward
    your passion, 131–33, 136–37, 142
resentment vs. anger, 64, 72, 79
sharing as key to freedom, 133–34,
    136, 138, 230
stress from anger, 130–31
successful people vs. failures, 132–33
tools for dealing with anger,
    139–41, 142
verbal violence, 126, 135, 136
"warped motivation," 131
what else can I assume about this?,
    133–34, 142
women vs. men, 130
See also children of domestic violence
Annabelle's story, 145–50, 161–62
answers for children of domestic
    violence, 16–20
See also From the Lie to the Truth
anxiety, 69
approval from others, need for, 169,
    210, 218
Argentina, 58, 59, 61
Arizona, 193
Ask (DATA: Decide, Ask, Truth, Act),
    103, 140–41, 142–43
assuming positive intent, 121, 123
Atlas Shrugged (Rand), 27
attractive. *See* self-conscious to
    attractive
awareness of children of domestic
    violence, 8–11, 22, 24, 151

Barrymore, Drew, 13
beauty, self-conscious to attractive, 218
beauty pageants, 191, 195, 196, 214, 215
"Behind Closed Doors" (UNICEF),
    6, 22
"benign neglect," 32
Benton, Tennessee, 155
Berry, Halle, 13
bitterness, resentful to compassionate,
    62–65, 68–69, 79

blame, taking away your power, 127–29
blood pressure, 69
Bodybuilding.com, 228, 229
body image. *See* self-conscious to
    attractive
body language and self-esteem,
    211–12, 215
*Boy Who Was Raised As a Dog and Other
    Stories from a Child Psychiatrist's
    Notebook, The* (Perry, Szalavitz), 6,
    58
Bradshaw, John, 28
brain impacted by domestic violence
    alone to trusting, 105, 112–13, 118–19
    angry to passionate, 126, 129–30, 133
    children of domestic violence, 7–8,
        15, 18, 24
    fearful to confident, 184–85, 199
    guilty to free, 27–28, 32–33, 42, 53
    resentful to compassionate, 68, 73
    sad to grateful, 98, 100
    self-conscious to attractive, 206
    unloved to loving, 232–33
    worthless to accomplished, 166–67
See also children of domestic violence
Brizendine, Louann, 130, 206
Broadway, 37
Brooklyn, New York, 115
Brown, Brené, 182
Brown, Margaret Wise, 231, 238–40
Brown, Scott, 13
bullying, 8, 130, 137, 186

Caribbean, 115
Carmel, California, 134
Caroline's story, 165–66, 167–73, 178
CDV (Children of Domestic Violence),
    xii, xviii, 45, 124, 245
Center on the Developing Child,
    Harvard University, 95
certainty of misery vs. misery of
    uncertainty, 83, 182
Change a Life program, 23
change creating momentum,
    24–25, 26
changing the pattern, angry to
    passionate, 134–36
Chelsea's story, 50–51
Chicago, Illinois, 173
child abuse vs. domestic violence, 9

Child Protective Services, 226
children, hearing it all, 207–8
Children Next Door, The (documentary),
    157, 183
children of domestic violence, xxi–xxii,
    1–26
    answers for, 16–20
    awareness of domestic violence, 8–11,
        22, 24, 151
    brain impacted by domestic violence,
        7–8, 15, 18, 24
    bullying associated with, 8, 130,
        137, 186
    change creating momentum,
        24–25, 26
    cognitive belief system (self-concept),
        8, 23–24, 132, 166–67, 179, 204
    controlling the meaning of your
        experiences, 16–19
    cycle of domestic violence, 2, 11, 12,
        13, 16
    defying the odds, 12–14
    happiness defined, 3
    health problems, 6–7, 30–31, 32–33,
        69, 85–86, 96
    impact of, 3, 6–8, 11
    learning from those who came
        before us, 25–26
    least popular ranking by
        peers, 114
    lies learned from, 3–4, 8, 23–24, 26
    living with domestic
        violence, 1–4
    nonphysical violence, greatest pain,
        173–74, 212–14, 218, 233
    One, the (helping to unlearn what
        was learned), 15–16, 23, 26
    predictor of becoming perpetrators
        or victims, 6
    resilience (invincibility), 14–16, 23,
        25, 241–46
    self-awareness and self-control, 4–6
    sharing as key to freedom, 245, 246
    silence about domestic violence, 9–10
    spiritual strength of, xv, 14, 74–75,
        80, 236
    statistics about, 2, 11, 12, 210
    undiscovered gifts, 3–4, 14–16, 23, 25
    "unlearning what was learned,"
        15–16, 24, 33

"witness," 9, 10–11
witnessing domestic violence as
    psychologically damaging as
    physical abuse, 4, 43
    See also brain impacted by domestic
        violence; cycle of domestic
        violence; lies learned by children
        of domestic violence; Martin,
        Brian F.; One, the (helping to
        unlearn what was learned);
        physical violence; sharing as key to
        freedom; verbal violence
Children of Domestic Violence (CDV),
    xii, xviii, 45, 124, 245
Child Trauma Academy in Houston, 223
Clinton, Bill, 1, 13, 73–74
Coelho, Paulo, 221
cognitive belief system (self-concept), 8,
    23–24, 132, 166–67, 179, 204
cold shoulder (silent treatment), 64,
    129, 170, 171
Columbia University, 114
compassion, 68–70, 72, 78–79, 80, 122
    See also resentful to compassionate
confidence, 189–91
    See also fearful to confident
confirmation bias, 98
control from anger, 129–31, 136–37, 141
controlling the meaning of your
    experiences, 16–19
controlling your anger, 137–38, 142
corpus callosum, 130
cortisol, 223
cortisone, 96
cost of anger, 136–37
courage, 182, 197, 198
Covey, Stephen, 19
Crystal's story, 5
"cuddle chemical" (oxytocin), 224
Cuddy, Amy, 196
cutting (self-injury), sad to grateful, 71,
    89–90, 91–92, 94
cycle of domestic violence, 2, 11, 12, 16
    alone to trusting, 115–16
    angry to passionate, 126
    fearful to confident, 187
    guilty to free, 38, 49–50
    hopeless to guided, 145, 155, 160
    resentful to compassionate, 60
    sad to grateful, 86, 93

self-conscious to attractive, 206,
  208, 209
unloved to loving, 232
worthless to accomplished, 168, 169,
  170, 172, 174
See also children of domestic violence
cytokine activity, 32–33

Dallas (TV show), 37
Dangerous Curves (movie), 37
DATA (Decide, Ask, Truth, Act), 103,
  140–41, 142–43
deciding on the outcomes that matter
  most, worthless to accomplished,
  178, 179–80
defying the odds, 12–14
demeaning words. See verbal violence
Department of Justice, 7
depression, 6, 32, 69, 85, 88, 96, 98,
  131, 157, 194
disappointment as personal affront,
  sad to grateful, 88
Doidge, Norman, 10, 18, 24, 133, 244
domestic violence, growing up with. See
  children of domestic violence
Dr. Phil (TV show), 45, 157
Drama Studio (London), 36
"Drop-Offs," 86–87
drug abuse. See substance abuse

eating disorders, 203, 204, 208, 213, 215
Eleanor's story, 105, 107–12, 118
eleven-plus exam (English school
  system), 34
Emily's story, 203–6, 207–10, 215–16
emotional abuse, 166
See also children of domestic violence
emotional thinking
  alone to trusting, 118–19
  guilty to free, 28, 52, 53
  sad to grateful, 98, 100
empathy, resentful to compassionate,
  61, 72, 76–77, 80–81, 122
England, post–World War II, 29, 31–32,
  34, 35–36
Europe, 86, 87, 91, 92

failure to thrive syndrome, 224
failures vs. successful people, 132–33
Faith's story, 38–43, 42–45

Family Refuge Center, 119, 227–28, 229
fault (your), guilty to free, 32–33,
  41–43, 46, 47, 48, 52, 53, 55, 57, 70
fearful to confident, 23, 24, 181–201
  brain and, 184–85, 199
  confidence, 189–91
  courage, 182, 197, 198
  cycle of domestic violence, 187
  From the Lie to the Truth, 199–201
  hesitation and uncertainty, 191–94
  hypervigilance state, 184
  keys to confidence, 195–97
  Olivia's story, 50, 183–91, 197
  other lies and, 204, 217, 221, 240, 242
  Payton's story, 191–97
  physical violence, 183, 186, 192, 193
  post-traumatic stress disorder
    (PTSD), 13, 161, 191, 193–94
  "power pose," 196, 201
  preparedness, 197–99, 200–201
  rescuing, hurting, 185–88
  sharing as key to freedom, 188–89,
    190, 196, 197, 198–99, 230
  survival instincts, 184–85, 190
  taking action, 188–89
  verbal violence, 186, 192–93
  See also children of domestic violence
Fields, R. Douglas, 68, 130
fight-or-flight reaction, 129, 131
finding purpose, hopeless to guided,
  149–50, 226
Fiona's story, 96–97, 98, 99–101
focusing on yourself and self-esteem,
  sad to grateful, 96–101, 103
forgiveness and healing, 60, 64–65,
  65–68, 75, 81, 228
Frames of the Mind: The Theory of Multiple
  Intelligences (Gardner), 154
Frankl, Viktor, 16–17, 18, 19, 152
free. See guilty to free
Freud's Last Session (off-Broadway
  show), 37
friendships, 113
From the Lie to the Truth, xxii
  alone to trusting, 122–24
  angry to passionate, 141–43
  fearful to confident, 199–201
  guilty to free, 53–55
  hopeless to guided, 163–64
  resentful to compassionate, 79–81

From the Lie to the Truth (*cont.*)
   sad to grateful, 101–3
   self-conscious to attractive, 218–19
   unloved to loving, 241–42
   worthless to accomplished, 178–80
   See also lies learned by children of
      domestic violence

Gandhi, Mahatma, 76
Gardner, Howard, 154
gateway to trust, 120–21
gender and anger, 130
gender and violence, 86–88
Georgia, 146, 150
goals, worthless to accomplished,
   169–71, 180
goodness at your core, resentful to
   compassionate, 76–79, 80
Goodnight Moon (Brown), 231, 238–40
good things don't happen to people
   like me, hopeless to guided,
   155–58
Gopnik, Alison, 3, 12, 122, 126
Graham-Bermann, Sandra, 48, 97–98,
   137, 139, 214
gratitude, 92–95, 99, 100, 101, 102
   See also sad to grateful
Gray, Albert E. N., 132
growing up with domestic violence. *See*
   children of domestic violence
guardian angel, becoming your
   own, 162
guided. *See* hopeless to guided
guilty to free, 23, 27–55
   addiction, guilt as, 38
   brain and, 27–28, 32–33, 42, 53
   cycle of domestic violence, 38, 49–50
   emotional thinking, 28, 52, 53
   Faith's story, 38–45
   fault (your), 32–33, 41–43, 46, 47, 48,
      52–53, 55, 57, 70
   From the Lie to the Truth, 53–55
   journaling, 45, 51–52, 55
   Martin Rayner's story, 29–32,
      34–37, 38
   One, the (helping to unlearn what
      was learned), 34–36, 44
   other lies, 204, 217, 221, 240–42
   physical violence, 29–30, 39, 40
   rational thinking, 28, 32, 38, 52, 53

sharing as key to freedom, 10, 38,
   39–41, 45–46, 47–50, 54, 230
something I could have done to stop
   it, 31–32, 33, 38, 46, 50, 52–53, 55
taking action, 28, 29, 36–37, 38,
   43–45, 45–46, 47, 50–53, 54
verbal violence, 30, 39
willpower, guilt as enemy of, 28, 38,
   48, 50, 51, 54, 217
   See also children of domestic violence
gun incident, 11–12, 16
Guy's story, 212, 213

happiness defined, 3
Harvard University, 95, 130, 184, 196
Healing the Shame That Binds You
   (Bradshaw), 28
health problems from domestic
   violence, 6–7, 30–31, 32–33, 69,
   85–86, 96
   See also specific problems
heart disease, 69
Hell Week, Navy SEALs, 127
helping to unlearn what was learned.
   See One, the
Hemingway, Ernest, 117
hesitation and uncertainty, 191–94
higher plane, resentful to
   compassionate, 14, 74–76, 80
hippocampus, 68
hopeless to guided, 23, 24, 145–64
   Annabelle's story, 145–50, 161–62
   Chelsea's story, 50–51, 155–60, 161,
      181
   cycle of domestic violence, 145,
      155, 160
   From the Lie to the Truth, 163–64
   good things don't happen to people
      like me, 155–58
   guardian angel, becoming your
      own, 162
   hopelessness, 85, 147, 149, 151, 163
   learned helplessness, 151
   multiple intelligences, 154–55
   other lies, 204, 217, 221, 240–42
   physical violence, 147, 153, 155, 156
   post-traumatic growth, 13, 161–62
   purpose, finding, 149–50, 226
   purpose for now, identifying your,
      158–60, 163, 164

school grades and intelligence, 152–54

sharing as key to freedom, 150, 158–59, 161, 230

verbal violence, 145, 146, 148

why we should be hopeful, 151–52

See also children of domestic violence

Houston, Texas, 69, 182, 223

How the Brain Learns (Sousa), 7

Hrdy, Sarah Blaffer, 61

hurting others, creating ultimate sadness, 95–96, 102, 103

hurting/rescuing, fearful to confident, 185–88

hypervigilance state, fearful to confident, 184

Idaho, 191

identifying your purpose for now, hopeless to guided, 158–60, 163, 164

Illinois, 173

immunological problems, 32–33, 69

India, 120

Indiana, 88, 134

inflammatory conditions, 32–33

insignificance and anger, 125, 129

insults. *See* verbal violence

intelligences, multiple, 154–55

intimacy, 106, 112, 121

intimidation, 168, 170

See also children of domestic violence

intuition skill (nonverbal communication), 58, 67–68

invincibility (resilience), 14–16, 23, 25, 241–46

See also children of domestic violence

Isle of Wight, 36

isolation. *See* alone to trusting

It's a Wonderful Life (movie), 162

Janine's story, 69–73, 75, 76

Jeremy's story, 125–29, 131–34, 139, 216

Joe's story, 175

Joseph, Stephen, 13, 45, 129, 161, 176

journaling, 45, 51–52, 55, 172, 173

Journey Through Emotional Abuse, A: From Bondage to Freedom (Caroline), 172

Julia's story, 114–18

Kahneman, Daniel, 161

keeping others at a distance, 111–13, 122

"keep running," 147

Keith's story, 1–2, 9, 11, 18, 46, 113, 198, 231, 238

Kids' Club, 48

knowing yourself and trusting, 114–20, 122, 123, 124

Law & Order (TV show), 37

learned helplessness, 151

learning from those who came before us, 25–26

least popular ranking by peers, 114

lies learned by children of domestic violence, 3–4, 8, 23–24, 26

From the Lie to the Truth, xxii

"unlearning what was learned," 15–16, 24, 33

See also alone to trusting; angry to passionate; children of domestic violence; fearful to confident; From the Lie to the Truth; guilty to free; hopeless to guided; Martin, Brian F.; One, the (helping to unlearn what was learned); resentful to compassionate; sad to grateful; self-conscious to attractive; unloved to loving; worthless to accomplished

life narrative, 121

liposuction, 216–17

living with domestic violence, 1–4

Lockridge story, the Roger "Rock," 216, 221–23, 224–30, 236

lost childhood, sad to grateful, 85–86, 93, 101, 102

love, understanding meaning of, 231–32

See also unloved to loving

Lyubomirsky, Sonja, 44, 45, 63, 101, 121, 147, 181, 188, 228

Madanes, Cloé, 14, 75, 145, 212

Makers of Memories, 21

Male Brain, The (Brizendine), 206

"Manage the Gap," 19

Mandela, Nelson, 57, 69

Man's Search for Meaning (Frankl), 16–17, 152
marijuana, 39–40
Marina's story, 58–63, 64, 65–67, 75
Martin, Brian F., xxi–xxii
  Change a Life program, 23
  childhood of, 1–2
  Children Next Door, The (documentary), 157, 183
  courage, 198–99
  friendships, 113
  gun incident, 11–12, 16
  liposuction, 216–17
  love, understanding meaning of, 231–32
  Makers of Memories, 21
  "Manage the Gap," 19
  metal shop and horse racing, 17–18
  mother's childhood of domestic violence, 16, 49–50
  mother's legacy of love: *Goodnight Moon* (Brown), 231, 238–40
  my wish for you, 243–46
  police station and pajamas, 9, 20
  prayers were never answered, 152–53
  professional success of, 20
  sharing as key to freedom, 47–48, 106, 198–99
  son lost in park, 77–78, 80
  Stacey (Brian's wife), 20, 106
  staying awake so I could take action, 46–47
  two a.m. visits by mother, 16–17
  See also children of domestic violence; lies learned by children of domestic violence
masking the pain of feeling unloved, 234–36
McDonald, Renee, xvii–xx, 9, 33, 161, 165
McGonigal, Kelly, 4, 19, 50, 223
McNally, Richard J., 42
meaning of your experiences, controlling, 16–19
memory, 10
men vs. women, angry to passionate, 130
metal shop and horse racing, 17–18
mind-body connection, 243
mindfulness, 19

mirror neuron system (MNS), 33, 112, 126, 206–7
misery of uncertainty vs. certainty of misery, 83, 182
Miss America pageant circuit, 191, 195, 196
MNS (mirror neuron system), 33, 112, 126, 206–7
Monroe, Marilyn, 203
Mort's story, 173–78
mother and infant connection, 223–24
Mother Teresa, 75
Muddy Creek Mountain, West Virginia, 221
multiple intelligences, 154–55
My Life (Clinton), 1
my wish for you, 243–46

naturopathy, 148, 149
Navy SEALs, 127, 133
Neff, Kristin, 19
negative intent assumption, 105, 112–13
neocortex, 28, 100, 184–85
Newark, New Jersey, 1, 216
Newark Star-Ledger, 17
New Hampshire, 97
New Jersey, 1, 157, 216
New Mexico, 71
New Orleans, 115
New York, 37, 96, 115
Nickelodeon, 21
nonphysical violence, greatest pain, 173–74, 212–14, 218, 233
  See also children of domestic violence
nonverbal communication (intuition skill), 58, 67–68
Nooyi, Indra, 120
North Carolina, 167
Northwestern University, 223
not good enough, worthless to accomplished, 168–69, 173–78, 178–79

Olivia's story, 50, 183–91, 197
One, the (helping to unlearn what was learned)
  alone to trusting, 108, 111
  children of domestic violence, 15–16, 23, 26
  guilty to free, 34–36, 44

resentful to compassionate, 65–67
sad to grateful, 93–94
"unlearning what was learned,"
  15–16, 24, 33
unloved to loving, 225
See also children of domestic
  violence; lies learned by children
  of domestic violence
Ontario, Canada, 38
Oprah Winfrey Show, The (TV show), 16
Oregon, 87, 92
Other Brain, The (Fields), 68
outcome vs. goal, worthless to
  accomplished, 26, 172–73, 180
oxytocin ("cuddle chemical"), 224

pageants (beauty), 191, 195, 196,
  214, 215
Paris, France, 239
passionate. *See* angry to passionate
passive aggressive behavior, 170
past (cutting ties with), resentful to
  compassionate, 69, 74, 75–76,
  78, 79
Payton's story, 191–97
Pennebaker, James, 33, 51–52
PepsiCo, 120
Perry, Bruce, 6, 15, 58, 83, 112, 182, 223
personality assessment, 119–20
Philosophical Baby, The (Gopnik), 126
physical violence, 5–6, 11
  alone to trusting, 107, 115
  angry to passionate, 125, 126,
    135, 136
  fearful to confident, 183, 186,
    192, 193
  guilty to free, 29–30, 39, 40
  hopeless to guided, 147, 153, 155, 156
  resentful to compassionate, 62, 63
  sad to grateful, 84, 88
  self-conscious to attractive, 207, 208
  unloved to loving, 222
  worthless to accomplished, 171, 175
  See also children of domestic violence
police station and pajamas, 9, 20
positive intent, assuming, 121, 123
post-traumatic growth, hopeless to
  guided, 13, 161–62
post-traumatic stress disorder (PTSD),
  13, 161, 191, 193–94

"power pose," 196, 201
prayers were never answered, 152–53
predictor of becoming perpetrators or
  victims of domestic violence, 6
prefrontal cortex, 68, 130
preparedness, fearful to confident,
  197–99, 200–201
procreation, 206
prostate cancer, 37
PTSD (post-traumatic stress disorder),
  13, 161, 191, 193–94
Public Theater, 37
Purpose Driven Life, The (Warren), 27
purpose (finding), hopeless to guided,
  149–50, 226
purpose for now, identifying your,
  hopeless to guided, 158–60,
  163, 164

Queens, New York, 115
questioning the anger, 134–36

Rand, Ayn, 27
Raoul's story, 59–60, 61–62, 63, 64,
  66, 67
rational thinking
  alone to trusting, 119
  guilty to free, 28, 32, 38, 52, 53
  sad to grateful, 100
Rayner, Martin's story, 29–32,
  34–37, 38
redirecting anger's energy toward your
  passion, 131–33, 136–37, 142
rejection fear, self-conscious to
  attractive, 215–17
relationships
  choices, self-conscious to attractive,
    206, 207, 208, 209, 213
  loss, unloved to loving, 222–23
  trust and, 105–6, 108, 109, 111,
    112, 122
"Report of the Attorney General's Task
  Force on Children Exposed
  to Violence" (Department of
  Justice), 7
rescuing/hurting, fearful to confident,
  185–88
resentful to compassionate, 23, 57–81
  anger vs. resentment, 64, 72, 79
  bitterness, 62–65, 68–69, 79

resentful to compassionate (*cont.*)
  brain and, 68, 73
  compassion, 68–70, 72, 78–79,
    80, 122
  cycle of domestic violence, 60
  empathy, 61, 72, 76–77, 80–81, 122
  forgiveness and healing, 60, 64–65,
    65–68, 75, 81, 228
  From the Lie to the Truth, 79–81
  goodness at your core, 76–79, 80
  higher plane, 14, 74–76, 80
  intuition skill (nonverbal
    communication), 58, 67–68
  Janine's story, 69–73, 75, 76
  Marina's story, 58–63, 64, 65–67, 75
  One, the (helping to unlearn what
    was learned), 65–67
  other lies, 204, 217, 221, 240–42
  past, cutting ties with, 69, 74, 75–76,
    78, 79
  physical violence, 62, 63
  sharing as key to freedom, 73,
    74, 230
  verbal violence, 60, 61, 62
  See also children of domestic violence
resilience (invincibility), 14–16, 23, 25,
    241–46
  See also children of domestic violence
Rhode Island, 185
risk taking, 106, 117, 118, 121, 123–24
Robbins, Tony, xi–xvi, 13, 125, 236
Robinson, Jackie, 243
Rowena's story, 83–84, 86–87, 87–88

sad to grateful, 23, 83–103
  adversity and happiness, 101
  brain and, 98, 100
  confirmation bias, 98
  cycle of domestic violence, 86, 93
  DATA (Decide, Ask, Truth, Act), 103,
    140–41, 142–43
  disappointment as personal
    affront, 88
  emotional thinking, 98, 100
  Fiona's story, 96–97, 98, 99–101
  focusing on yourself and self-esteem,
    96–101, 103
  From the Lie to the Truth, 101–3
  gender and violence, 86–88
  gratitude, 92–95, 99, 100, 101, 102
    hurting others, creating ultimate
      sadness, 95–96, 102, 103
  lost childhood, 85–86, 93, 101, 102
  One, the (helping to unlearn what
    was learned), 93–94
  other lies, 204, 217, 221, 240–42
  physical violence, 84, 88
  rational thinking, 100
  Savannah's story, 83–84, 86–95, 101
  self-injury (cutting), 71, 89–90,
    91–92, 94
  sharing as key to freedom, 94, 230
  stress, biochemistry of, 95–96
  verbal violence, 84, 87
  See also children of domestic violence
Salem, Virginia, 228
sarcasm. *See* verbal violence
Savannah, Georgia, 146, 150
Savannah's story, 83–84, 86–95, 101
Schechter, Daniel, 114
Schindler, John, 3, 243
school grades and intelligence, 152–54
screaming. *See* verbal violence
Seattle, Washington, 93
self-awareness and self-control, 4–6
self-concept (cognitive belief system), 8,
    23–24, 132, 166–67, 179, 204
self-conscious to attractive, 23, 24,
    203–19
  approval from others, need for, 169,
    210, 218
  body language and self-esteem,
    211–12, 215
  brain and, 206
  children, hearing it all, 207–8
  cycle of domestic violence, 206,
    208, 209
  eating disorders, 203, 204, 208,
    213, 215
  Emily's story, 203–6, 207–10,
    215–16
  From the Lie to the Truth, 218–19
  key to being attractive, 217
  mirror neuron system (MNS), 33,
    112, 126, 206–7
  nonphysical violence, greatest pain,
    173–74, 212–14, 218, 233
  other lies, 221, 240, 242
  physical violence, 207, 208
  rejection, fear of, 215–17

relationship choices and, 206, 207, 208, 209, 213
sharing as key to freedom, 209, 230
Suzanne's story, 212–14, 215–16
transforming the lie, 214–15
understanding why we feel self-conscious, 209–10, 218
unloved to loving, 227–28
validation, receiving as child, 214
verbal violence, 210–11, 213, 214
wearing our pain on the outside, 210–12
self-esteem, 6, 243–44
body language, self-conscious to attractive, 211–12, 215
focusing on yourself and self-esteem, sad to grateful, 96–101, 103
low self-esteem, worthless to accomplished, 166–68
self-injury (cutting), sad to grateful, 71, 89–90, 91–92, 94
self-worth for your children, worthless to accomplished, 177–78, 180
separation anxiety, 223–24
Seven Habits of Highly Effective People, The (Covey), 19
sexual abuse, 70–71
See also children of domestic violence
Shakespeare in the Park, New York, 37
shame, toxic, 28
See also guilty to free
sharing as key to freedom
alone to trusting, 106, 110, 230
angry to passionate, 133–34, 136, 138, 230
children of domestic violence, 245, 246
fearful to confident, 188–89, 190, 196, 197, 198–99, 230
guilty to free, 10, 38, 39–41, 45–46, 47–50, 54, 230
hopeless to guided, 150, 158–59, 161, 230
Martin, Brian F., 47–48, 106, 198–99
resentful to compassionate, 73, 74, 230
sad to grateful, 94, 230
self-conscious to attractive, 209, 230
unloved to loving, 228–30, 237, 242
worthless to accomplished, 172–73, 230
See also children of domestic violence

Shonkoff, Jack P., 95–96, 184
silence about domestic violence, 9–10
silent treatment (cold shoulder), 64, 129, 170, 171
sleep disturbances, 96
social need of humans, unloved to loving, 223, 241
society's basic moral value (trust), 121
something I could have done to stop it, guilty to free, 31–32, 33, 38, 46, 50, 52–53, 55
son lost in park, 77–78, 80
Sousa, David
cognitive belief system (self-concept), 8, 166–67
emotional brain of children, 32, 118–19
false conclusions by children, 46
How the Brain Learns (Sousa), 7
loving behavior, parents as role models, 232–33
mirror neuron system (MNS), 112
negative intent assumption, 105, 112–13
neocortex and rational brain, 28, 184–85
society's basic moral value (trust), 121
survival mode, 184–85
"unlearning what was learned," 15
Southern Methodist University, xx, 33, 165
spiritual strength of children of domestic violence, xv, 14, 74–76, 80, 236
Star Trek (TV show and movies), 37
statistics about children of domestic violence, 2, 11, 12, 210
staying awake so I could take action, 46–47
Stewart, Jimmy, 162
Stewart, Patrick, 13
Stiles, William, 45
Strategic Family Therapy, 212
stress, biochemistry of, 95–96
stress from anger, 130–31
substance abuse, 11, 12, 69, 86, 91, 135, 145, 177, 204, 207, 222, 225
successful people vs. failures, 132–33
suicide, 11, 91, 93, 173, 193

survival instincts, fearful to confident, 184–85, 190

survival machines (humans), worthless to accomplished, 176, 179–80

suspicions of others, 118–19

Suzanne's story, 212–14, 215–16

"tact and tone" problem, 94

Talk Radio (movie), 37

Tamil Nadu, India, 120

temporal parietal junction system (TPJ), 206

Tennessee, 155, 171

testosterone, 130

Texas, 33, 69, 182, 223

tools for dealing with anger, 139–41, 142

Torre, Joe, 13

toxic shame, 28
    See also guilty to free

TPJ (temporal parietal junction system), 206

transforming the lie, self-conscious to attractive, 214–15

trauma-related symptoms, 6

trust and knowing yourself, 114–20, 122, 123, 124
    See also alone to trusting

truth
    DATA (Decide, Ask, Truth, Act), 103, 140–41, 142–43
    See also From the Lie to the Truth

Turner, Tina, 13

Twain, Mark, 197

UK study on self-harm, 89

ulcers, 32, 37, 69

ultimate truth of love, 237

undeserved guilt (accepting), worst guilt, 27

undiscovered gifts, 3–4, 14–16, 23, 25

UNICEF, 2, 6, 22

University of California, Berkeley, 3, 122

University of California, Los Angeles, 32–33

University of Houston, 182

University of Michigan, 48, 97

University of Texas, 33

"unlearning what was learned," 15–16, 24, 33

See also children of domestic violence; lies learned by children of domestic violence; One, the (helping to unlearn what was learned)

unloved to loving, 23, 24, 221–42
    acknowledging regrets and commitment to new pursuits, 228
    Amanda's story, 232, 233–34, 235–36
    brain and, 232–33
    cycle of domestic violence, 232
    failure to thrive syndrome, 224
    From the Lie to the Truth, 241–42
    love, understanding meaning of, 231–32
    masking the pain of feeling unloved, 234–36
    mother and infant connection, 223–24
    One, the (helping to unlearn what was learned), 225
    other lies and, 204, 217
    physical violence, 222
    relationship loss, 222–23
    Roger "Rock" Lockridge's story, 216, 221–23, 224–30, 236
    self-conscious, becoming less, 227–28
    separation anxiety, 223–24
    sharing as key to freedom, 228–30, 237, 242
    social need of humans, 223, 241
    ultimate truth of love, 237
    verbal violence, 222, 234
    See also children of domestic violence

validation, receiving as child, 214

verbal violence, 4–5
    alone to trusting, 115
    angry to passionate, 126, 135, 136
    fearful to confident, 186, 192–93
    guilty to free, 30, 39
    hopeless to guided, 145, 146, 148
    resentful to compassionate, 60, 61, 62
    sad to grateful, 84, 87
    self-conscious to attractive, 210–11, 213, 214
    unloved to loving, 222, 234
    worthless to accomplished, 170, 171, 174, 175
    See also children of domestic violence

Victor Victoria (movie), 37
Vietnam War, 125
Virginia, 145, 228
vulnerability, 111

Waldroup, Chelsea, 50–51,
 155–60, 161, 181
Walt Disney World in Florida, 21, 22
Walter's story, 125, 126
"warped motivation," 131
Warren, Rick, 27, 60, 64, 65, 169, 185
Washington State, 93, 165
wearing our pain on the outside, self-
 conscious to attractive, 210–12
West Virginia, 221
*What Doesn't Kill Us: The New Psychology
 of Post-Traumatic Growth* (Joseph),
 45, 161, 176
what else can I assume about this?,
 angry to passionate, 133–34, 142
willpower, guilt as enemy of, 28, 38, 48,
 50, 51, 54, 217
Windsor, Ontario, 38
Winfrey, Oprah, 13
"Wishes" (fireworks show), 21
"witness," 9, 10–11
witnessing domestic violence as
 psychologically damaging as
 physical abuse, 4, 43
women vs. men, angry to
 passionate, 130
workaholism, 234

worthless to accomplished, 23, 24,
 165–80
 approval from others, need for, 169,
  210, 218
 brain and, 166–67
 Caroline's story, 165–66, 167–73, 178
 cycle of domestic violence, 168, 169,
  170, 172, 174
 deciding on the outcomes that
  matter most, 178, 179–80
 From the Lie to the Truth, 178–80
 goals, 169–71, 180
 journaling, 172, 173
 low self-esteem, 166–68
 Mort's story, 173–78
 not good enough, 168–69, 173–78,
  178–79
 other lies, 204, 217, 221, 240–242
 outcome vs. goal, 26, 172–73, 180
 physical violence, 171, 175
 self-worth for your children,
  177–78, 180
 sharing as key to freedom,
  172–73, 230
 survival machines, humans as, 176,
  179–80
 verbal violence, 170, 171, 174, 175
 See also children of domestic
  violence
"writing paradigm," 51–52
 See also journaling
Wrosch, Carsten, 68–69

ABOUT THE AUTHOR

Brian F. Martin grew up living with domestic violence. The impact lasted into adulthood. This pain drove him to seek answers, which eventually led to a revelation that uncovered the gifts that the experience left behind—the hidden truths earned along the way for anyone who grew up in a home like his.

He applied those truths and began living a life that was closer to his full potential. By creating multimillion-dollar global enterprises, a deep connection with his two young children, a healthy and vital body, a confident mind-set that he controlled, and loving relationships, he unlearned the lies and reinforced the truths of his life. Truths that he realized are the birthright of anyone who grew up living with domestic violence—all one billion alive today.

With this in mind, he created CDV—Children of Domestic Violence, an international nonprofit organization created to connect and support anyone who grew up living with domestic violence as they strive to reach the full potential they were destined to realize.

To learn more about Children of Domestic Violence, visit cdv.org.